The Greatest Craftsman

This book is set in the typeface *Athelas* designed by Veronika Burian and Jose Scaglione.

Paperback ISBN: 979-8-3672-5671-0
Hardcover ISBN: 978-1-0880-1008-2

A Publication of *Tall Pine Books*
119 E Center Street, Suite B4A | Warsaw, Indiana 46580
www.tallpinebooks.com

| 1 22 22 20 16 02 |

Published in the United States of America

The Greatest Craftsman

God's Divine Poem in a Woman's Purpose

Jacquie R. Maldonado

DEDICATION

To my mother, Alma: I thank God for giving me you, a mother who raised me in the way of our Abba. I thank you for being a mother who prayed for me without ceasing. If not for your fervent prayers, I would not have written this book. You are a true woman of God! I love you with all that I am. To my Uncle Marvin: Words cannot express what you mean to me. I'd like to express my gratitude for your unwavering support and all that you have done for me. And for being the Mordecai who pushed me to do God's will. You have imparted copious blessings into my life, and I have learned a great deal from you.

CONTENTS

CHAPTER 1: THE COMPOSER OF YOUR LIFE

God is the Creator of all things, and all things are created with a purpose. Your Composer, God, has all control.

CHAPTER 2: COCREATORS

God has created us in His image. We are animated to mirror the Greatest Craftsman. There is a potential in you that you can tap into.

CHAPTER 3: IDENTITY FORTIFIED

We all have identity issues. But when we come into God, our identity is found in Him and becomes fortified in the one who created us.

CHAPTER 4: RECONSTRUCTED MIND

Our minds can be renewed by the washing of God's Word. We can learn how to bring down the strongholds in our minds.

CHAPTER 5: GENETIC CODE TRANSFORMED

When we are reborn in Christ, we take on a new

DNA. Generational trauma and generational curses are removed through the blood of Jesus.

CHAPTER 6: THE THRESHING FLOOR

We are like wheat that must go through the process to bring forth that which is good. A threshing floor is a place for testing. We all enter into the Greatest Craftsman's threshing floor before He can entrust us with what He has crafted us for. This is where we learn to trust Him, rely on Him, and submit to Him.

CHAPTER 7: KINSHIP

Relationships are the currency of heaven. Like Ruth, we become part of the bloodline of Christ through relationships. Associations are crafted into your life as a key to help you enter into your purpose.

CHAPTER 8: IMAGINATION MADE REALITY

God has placed within you dreams that reflect His purpose and plans for you. He wants to make your dreams a reality.

CHAPTER 9: CARRY INTO ACTION

We can learn to move from hoping into doing. Jesus's mother did not just hope He would do something about the wine running out at the wedding: she took action. Show me your work and you show me your faith. We should learn to move by faith to bring change.

CHAPTER 10: MUSING WOMEN LEADERS

It's time for transformation. Answer the call. Set the stage for the Greatest Craftsman to be displayed in your life.

PREFACE

LIKE MANY WOMEN, I've had challenges. My father left the family when I was a child, which made me feel abandoned and rejected. I sought love in all the wrong places. Every relationship I had was tainted with infidelity, verbal and physical abuse, betrayal, and disappointment. My sense of self-worth vanished. Believing I was the problem, I felt trapped. I would try to make progress only to have three steps go wrong. I always believed there had to be more to life.

Eventually I reached the point where I couldn't take it anymore, so I cried out to God for help. He showed me what love is and who I am in Him. He shifted my mindset as I spent time in His Word and prayer. He showed me things in the Scripture that highlighted His messages to women.

After five years, an urge to write stirred in me.

Something I had never dreamed of. As I pondered what I would write about, He gave me revelations. The Spirit of our Lord revealed to me that this is the moment for women to rise because the empowerment and favor of the Lord is upon us.

As I boldly put my hands to the plow, His word came forth, and this book was born.

INTRODUCTION

G OD WANTS WOMEN to discover who they are in Christ and how to use the various talents He has endowed them with. God is the Greatest Craftsman, and He has crafted everything for a certain purpose. I believe God is raising an army of Musing Women Leaders for the season ahead. He is calling us to come forth and fight on the front lines.

Before we can answer the call, we must first be enabled. This book is designed to work alongside the Holy Spirit to empower you to stand up.

For many decades, women have been oppressed by society. However, God has equipped us with a mission and granted us the ability and authority to complete it. It is time for us to resume our rightful positions in the Kingdom of God.

In order to walk in the fullness of your vocation, certain bindings must be broken from your life. As you read this book, you will experience a renewing of your mind and a shifting of your thoughts. The identity crisis will break off your life, and the blood of Jesus will become your source of existence. You will be changed and restored to God's intended purpose.

It's the moment to break out of your limitations, and fulfill the plans God has for you.

CHAPTER ONE

The COMPOSER
of YOUR LIFE

All things were made by him; and without him was not any thing made that was made. John 1:3 KJV

GOD IS THE Creator of all things, and all things were created with a purpose. He holds all creation and makes Himself responsible for it. He is the Composer of all His creations. He has written in the Scripture. Acts 17:28 says, "For in him we live, and move, and have our being; as certain also of your own poets have said, For we are also his offspring." Before you can fully comprehend who you are, you must first grasp the wonderful Composer of your life.

The words of the Greatest Craftsman will set you free. Take time to consider them. Nothing is more powerful than hearing God Himself speak to you through His own words.

Let me share with you some of my favorite Scripture passages and what they mean to me.

Colossians 1:16–17 says, "For by him were all things created, that are in heaven, and that are in earth, visible and invisible, whether they be thrones, or dominions, or principalities, or powers: all things were created by him, and for him: And he is before all things, and by him all things consist."

God certainly knows how to take care of His creations. He's the Composer of your life, whose orchestration you have been commissioned to play—even if you don't understand it, now or ever!

The Bible refers to God as the Great I AM. He is the eternally self-existent one, independent of any other person or thing, existing without beginning or end (John 1:1; 8:58; Hebrews 13:8). He is the Great I AM in a unique way for every theme of your life and every day of the year.

These are just some of the names of God:

- I AM the God of wonders (Psalm 40:5)
- I AM the Lord with a powerful voice (Psalm 29:3-9)
- I AM God of the impossible (Luke 18:27)
- I AM a God of remembrance (Genesis 8:1,

Genesis 19:29)
- I AM the God of glory (Romans 3:23, Isaiah 42:8)
- I AM the God of wisdom and understanding (Proverbs 2:6, Daniel 2:20)
- I AM the Holy Spirit (John 14: 16-17, Matthew 28:19, John 4:24)
- I AM worthy of worship (John 4:23)
- I AM the God who makes myself known (Psalm 19:1-2)
- I AM the giver and taker (Job 1:21)
- I AM he who ascended (John 3:13)
- I AM the God who performs signs (Isaiah 7:14)
- I AM the Lord of Host (Psalm 24:10)
- I AM the God who searches (Jeremiah 17:10)
- I AM the great one (Isaiah 12:6)
- I AM Yahweh (Isaiah 50:10)
- I AM the Revelator (Deuteronomy 29:29)
- I AM hope (Psalm 54:4)
- I AM love (1 John 4:16)
- I AM the Good Shepherd (John 10:11)
- I AM your Advocate (1Timothy 2:5)
- I AM your Abba Father (Romans 8:15)
- I AM Immanuel, God with you (Isaiah 7:14)
- I AM the Master (Matthew 10:25)

- I AM strong (Job 9:19)
- I AM the Savior (Isaiah 43:11)
- I AM knowledge (Clossians 1:10)
- I AM omniscient (Proverbs 15:3)
- I AM the Great Healer (Exodus 23:25-26)
- I AM He who declares (Isaiah 40:21)
- I AM the answer (Isaiah 41:17)
- I AM prophecy fulfilled (Matthew 1:22)
- I AM the Giver of good gifts (James 1:17)
- I AM the God of symbols (Genesis 9:13)
- I AM He who is found (Isaiah 55:6-7)
- I AM the anointed oil (1 John 2:20)
- I AM the Living Water of life (Jeremiah 2:13)
- I AM the trumpet (1 Thessalonians 4:16)
- I AM the fountain (Psalm 36:8-9)
- I AM the living star (Revelation 22:16)
- I AM the Passover Lamb (John 1:29)
- I AM the ark of the covenant (Exodus 25:22)
- I AM the door (John 10:9)
- I AM the tree of life (Revelation 2:7)
- I AM the Lily of the Valley (Song of Solomon 2:1)
- I AM the glory (Isaiah 42:8)
- I AM the cloud (Psalm 78:14)
- I AM the fire (Hebrew 12:29)
- I AM the Bread of Life (John 6:35)
- I AM the eternal one (1 Timothy 1:17)

- I AM your rock (Deuteronomy 32:4)
- I AM the Light of the World (John 8:12)
- I AM your promoter (1 Peter 5:6-7)
- I AM the God of mercy (Psalm 86:5)
- I AM favor and I give favor (Psalm 90:17)
- I AM the Prince of Peace (Isaiah 9:6)
- I AM your restorer (Jeremiah 30:17)
- I AM a friend of sinners (Mark 2:13-17)
- I AM a weeper (Jeremiah 9:10)
- I AM longsuffering (Deuteronomy 32:35)
- I AM gracious (2 Chronicles 30:9b)
- I AM the forgiver (Psalm 86:5)
- I AM the Son of God who came down from heaven (John 6:38)
- I AM the beloved of God the Father (Matthew 3:17)
- I AM the Holy One (Isaiah 43:15)
- I AM faithful (2 Timothy 2:13)

I pray that God reveals Himself to you as the Great I AM for whatever you need right now. There is no one like Him on earth, above the earth, or under the earth (1 Kings 8:23).

In John 18:5–6, Jesus Christ said, "I AM He," alluding to God's statement to Moses, "I AM THAT I AM," in Exodus 3:14. The name suggests eternity, not hindered by time. Jesus is the all-knowing God. And He lives within each of us.

"In the beginning was the Word, and the Word was with God, and the Word was God. The same was in the beginning with God. All things were made by him; and without him was not any thing made that was made" (John 1:1-3). *Jesus is the word. "And the Word was made flesh, and dwelt among us, (and we beheld his glory, the glory as of the only begotten of the Father,) full of grace and truth"* (John 1:14).

The Great I AM is the triune God: Father, Son, and Holy Spirit. He is forever present from generation to generation. He is three in one and all in one. All you need is Him.

In 2 Corinthians 4:7, we see Christ as the image of God, the full expression of who God is in all His attributes and virtues. Like God, Jesus loves and is love. He has wisdom and purpose. He can think, consider, like and dislike, and have intentions.

The Composer of your life has a soul. Isaiah 1:14 says, "Your new moons and your appointed feasts my *soul* hateth: they are a trouble unto me; I am weary to bear them."

God is righteous in His nature (2 Corinthians 5:21). His Son, Jesus, is righteous in all His ways

(John 1:1). Righteousness is characterized by uprightness and morality.

Nothing unjust or sinful dwells in God's habitation. The righteousness of God is evident in all His doings. According to Romans 3:10–12, no one but God is righteous.

According to Psalm 45:6, Jesus Christ rules by righteousness: "Thy throne, O God, is for ever and ever: the scepter of thy kingdom is a right scepter." And Job says, "God weighs everything in the scales of righteousness" (Job 31:6).

Psalm 89:14 says, "Justice and judgment are the habitation of thy throne: mercy and truth shall go before thy face." We have received forgiveness from God through his loving-kindness because His righteousness has been satisfied by the death of Jesus Christ on our behalf. As Isaiah wrote, "All we like sheep have gone astray; we have turned every one to his own way; and the Lord hath laid on him the iniquity of us all" (Isaiah 53:6).

God's method and standard of justice are based on His actions and character. He works by means of perfect standards and carries out justice with no unfairness. He will always judge things with an absolute standard, according to the truth.

God has demonstrated His righteousness through His sinless ways and Jesus's sacrifice on the cross. He didn't have any sin, but every one of us has sinned (Romans 3:23). He did not deserve death, but He willingly died a criminal's death (and worse) to show God's perfect justice.

Everything about God is truthful and just, which gives us peace. We can be certain that nothing will happen outside of His standard of justice and that everything will turn out for our good (Romans 8:28).

God's perfect will might be hard to comprehend sometimes, but we should not try to change it based on our own limited human wisdom. If we base our lives on His righteousness, measuring it with the truth, we won't need to fear anything.

God the Holy One

God is the Holy One in and by Himself (Isaiah 11:9), and in Him everything righteous lives and moves and has its being (Acts 17:28). God creates, saves, and makes all things holy. Each of His creatures owes its very existence to Him. There is no wrong in Him; everything He does is out of purity. There are no ulterior motives in Him, only holiness and glory. God's holiness governs everything. Leviticus 19:2 says, "Speak unto all the congregation of the children of Israel, and say unto them,

Ye shall be holy: for I the Lord your God am holy."

What does it mean that the Lord is holy? Let's dig deeper and find out what that means. According to Dictionary.com, holy means "set apart, consecrated." *Holy One* is an expression applied to God and Messiah (Isaiah 43:15; John 6:69). The Bible uses the word *holy* to describe people, places, and things that are dedicated to God's purpose. Mountains, hills, valleys, springs, even city walls may be called holy when used for God. God is holy because He is different from everything in creation. He is set apart and can stand alone.

In the beginning, there was nothing but darkness and God. The Lord was alone, existing in a state of absolute completeness. There was nothing to compare Himself with. He did not need anything or anyone. But He did desire, and He did make choices.

The darkness was without form and void (Genesis 1:1-2), simply dark matter and energy. The Lord's thoughts penetrated the darkness to bring forth light. He created boundaries between light and darkness. This was the purest, whitest light that has ever been seen or imagined.

God the Healer

God is the healer of all things (Exodus 15:26). He has provided for all of His creation and has special blessings for those who seek Him (1 John 5:14). By Jesus's stripes we are healed (Isaiah 53:5). Notice it doesn't say you *can be* healed, but you *are* healed. The stripes of Christ make our wounds disappear. We have been healed from within because God loves us so much.

God heals the brokenhearted, binding up their wounds (Psalm 147:3). He brings healing not only to our bodies but also to our hearts and minds. He takes away our pain (Micah 7:19), for He bore our pain on the day He was crucified.

The Lord is your physician (Exodus 15:2). This scripture was not only for the people of Israel in the Old Testament. This word still stands true today. The Lord is good to all, and His compassion is over everything that He has made (Psalm 145:9).

Seek Him and strive to experience Him intimately. The Great I AM is everything you need Him to be. All you have to do is let Him in.

God the Provider

Jesus Christ provides life and breath, joy and peace, guidance, clothing, health, food, comfort, power, and strength. Your heavenly Father wants to give the best gifts to you because you are His. He provided His Son so that whoever believes in Him would not perish but have eternal life (John 3:16). His name is Yahweh Yireh, meaning "The Lord Will Provide" (Genesis 22:14).

God provided all that we will ever need before the foundation of the world. And He has given us a new covenant, better than what we His children had through Moses. Come into His divine provision for your life, and you will have everything you need. Trust Him as your provider, and see how He multiples your provision.

Ask Him for what you want as well. God lacks nothing. He has in abundance, and He gives in abundance. He loves giving good gifts to His children.

God the Redeemer

God is the Redeemer of all things. What we think is lost He will restore in double portions (Isaiah 61:7).

God has a plan for those who love Him, and He is working it out in your life right now. Jeremiah 29:11 tells us, "For I know the thoughts that I think toward you, saith the Lord, thoughts of peace, and not of evil, to give you an expected end." He has a vision for your life. He has a target for you to follow. He has made a blueprint for you individually. He has thought it out and mapped it out.

God has a plan for all of His creation, and He works within His creation to fulfill His desires. God did not create the world and humanity by accident or haphazardly, but with an overall plan in mind for each person who comes into existence.

Job 42:2 says this about God: "I know that you can do anything, and no one can stop you" (NLT).

Jeremiah 32:19 says, "Great in counsel, and mighty in work: for thine eyes are open upon all the ways of the sons of men: to give every one according to his ways, and according to the fruit of his doings:"

Isaiah 46:10–11 says, "Declaring the end from the beginning, and from ancient times the things that are not yet done, saying, My counsel shall stand, and I will do all my pleasure: Calling a ravenous bird from the east, the man that executeth my counsel from a far country: yea, I have spoken it, I will also bring it to pass; I have purposed it, I will also do it."

God's will is His desire and plan, and His purpose carries out His will. The purpose is the tool He uses to fulfill His will. It delivers the outcome. The will is the highway, and the purpose is the vehicle you ride to carry out His plan. Everything in your life will serve a purpose: to get you to your destination, which is the will of God.

The will of God is to give life in abundance. To break the bonds of wickedness. To break the schemes of the enemy upon the earth. His purpose is unique for every individual. Each of us plays a specific role in God's divine masterpiece. "And we know that in all things God works for the good of those who love Him, who have been called according to His purpose" (Romans 8:28).

God is Sovereign

God is the authority and God has ultimate authority over all things. He works out everything for His eternal purpose (Ephesians 3:20; 1 Corinthians 2:7). God is sovereign. He has supreme power and authority.

The Bible tells us that all power comes from and is under the control of God (Isaiah 40:29-3; Romans 13:1). He is the origin of authority in the cosmos. In the beginning, God created the heavens and the earth (Genesis 1:1), and those things will end with Him being all in all (1 Corinthians 15:28). He spoke everything into existence. The universe does not operate independently from its

Creator. It is subject to Him and has always been since the beginning of time.

Nothing happens without God's authority. And nothing can stop what God is doing, because no one, nor anything, has control over Him.

In John 19:11, Jesus told Pilate, "Thou couldest have no power at all against me, except it were given thee from above: therefore he that delivered me unto thee hath the greater sin."

In Matthew 28:18, Jesus said, "All power is given unto me in heaven and in earth."

The Wisdom of God

God has intellect, and He is all-knowing. Romans 11:36 tells us that God has given us the very capacity to believe in Him.

God has perfect knowledge of all things, and He foresees everything before it happens. He is the Author of all that goes on in time and space. He knows what you are going to do, where you are going to go, whom you are going to meet, and what you are going to say or even think.

Our omniscient God is not surprised or caught off guard by anything. He is never taken by surprise, and He never has to alter His plans as a result of anything we do.

He knows what will happen until the end

of time itself. And it all happens according to a master plan that He proposed in Christ Jesus our Lord (Ephesians 1:11). He knows the end from the beginning.

God knows what will happen in the future, and He sometimes foretells using prophecy. The Bible is a prophetic book. He also has prophets today who release His word, foretelling what God tells them to say.

God Is Always Creating

God paints the skies every morning. Every moment is impregnated with the creativity of God. Every human mind has an imprinted image of God's creativity. Each day a child is born, which means God is bringing to life at every moment. Just look around you, and you will see how God is always creating in your life. He makes something out of nothing.

God is the Creator of everything in the universe. He is very creative, and His creativity is evident in all that He has made. For example, God created the stars, planets, and galaxies. He also created human beings, animals, and plants. Each of these things is unique and beautiful in its own way. God's creativity is also evident in the way He has designed the world. For instance, the world is full of variety, with different cultures, climates, and ecosystems. This variety makes the world an interesting and exciting place to live. God's creativity is also evident in the way He works in our lives. He often uses unexpected events and circumstances to teach us important lessons. In conclusion, God is a very creative being, and His creativity is evident in all that He has made.

He continues to create every day. Each flower that blooms is a testimony to His creative power. Even the simplest things, like a bird's song or a child's laughter, are evidence of His ongoing creativity. As we behold the beauty of His creation, let us remember that it is all a reflection of His glory. And let us also remember that we are His handiwork, created in His image to reflect His love and goodness to the world.

God Is Love

1 John 3:1 says, "Behold, what manner of love the Father hath bestowed upon us, that we should be called the sons of God: therefore the world knoweth us not, because it knew him not."

1 John 4:8 says, "He that loveth not knoweth not God; for God is love."

1 John 4:19 says, "We love him, because he first loved us."

God loves each of us so much that He will leave the ninety-nine who are doing well to go find the one who has been lost (Luke 15:4). We will never fully understand His love, as no man has ever loved the way He does. This love overwhelms us and draws us to Him.

All of this and more are contained within God's Great I AM-ness. And He has many other names and titles. If you want to know Him more, get into the Word of God so that He can reveal to you things you have never seen or heard. He will unveil who you are in Him.

The Composer of your life has created a song for you to play on the earth through your life. He has begun the work for you, and He will finish it (Philippians 1:6). And the glory will all be unto Him.

Too often, we think of love as a feeling that comes and goes. We fall in and out of love, we have good days and bad days. But what if love was something more than that? What if love was something that never wavered, no matter what we did or how we felt? That's the kind of love God has for us. His love is constant and unchanging, even when we screw up or turn our backs on Him. In fact, God's love is so strong that it led Him to send His only Son to die for our sins. That's how much

He loves us! So when we say that "God is love," we're not just talking about a sentimental feeling—we're talking about an unending, rock-solid commitment that will never falter, no matter what.

The Big Question

Jesus asked His disciples, "Who do you say that I am?" (Matthew 16:15). Every human being on earth has to answer this question for themselves. Your answer will reveal less about who He is than about who you are.

Who is Jesus to you right now? The answer to that question can be complex and personal. Perhaps you see Him as a guide, leading you on your spiritual journey. Maybe you view Him as a friend, someone you can turn to in times of need. Or maybe He is something more, someone who represents the very best of what it means to be human. Whoever Jesus is to you, know that He wants you to identify who He is and who you are to Him. So take some time to reflect on your relationship with Him. What does He mean to you? And what do you mean to Him? These are important questions worth exploring.

Who does God say that you are? To Him you

are a new creation, a reborn being of His workmanship. He designed and built you with a specific purpose for His glory. Do not allow your circumstances to identify who you truly are. There are facts in the circumstances around you but that doesn't necessarily mean that it is true. You are more than what has happened to you and or is happening to you. If it doesn't line up with what God says about who you are in Him and to Him, then the facts are not the truth.

You are meant to partner with your Composer. Be the instrument He plays to bring forth all He is and all you are. What instrument are you? What notes are you called to play? What sound do you carry? The Great I AM is the Composer of your life. Therefore you cannot be stopped. Do not allow the tribulations of life to paralyze you and keep you from becoming all He has designed you to be. Therefore, keep moving forward in faith, knowing that He has a good plan for you.

Declaration

Stop here and make this declaration out loud: God realigns me to His flawless will and objectives for my life. May I carry the sound of heaven in my divine written poem. Amen.

CHAPTER TWO

CO-CREATORS

*Verily, verily, I say unto you, He that believeth
on me, the works that I do shall he do also; and
greater works than these shall he do; because
I go unto my Father. And whatsoever ye shall
ask in my name, that will I do, that the Father
may be glorified in the Son. If ye shall ask any
thing in my name, I will do it. (John 14:12–14)*

DO YOU EVER wonder what you're doing
in this world? You're not alone. Many of us
have yet to discover who we really are. The truth
is, each of us is constantly evolving into the person God destined us to be. We move from glory
to glory, which implies that we will always be
changing until the coming of our Savior, Jesus
Christ. The purpose God has placed in us grows
as we progress through life. The answer to who
we are is found in God and God alone.

Animated to Mirror Him

God's Spirit animates us to mirror Him, and His power enables us to mirror Him. In other words He gives us life and the ability to reflect Him in our lives.

Jesus gave us the perfect example of what it looked like to animate our Father. He said, "I only do that which I see the Father do (John 5:19) and I only say that which I hear the Father say" (John 8:38). Since we have the same spirit that was in Jesus, we can mirror God just as Jesus did when He walked the earth. Not by our own strength, but by the power of the Holy Spirit, we are capable of living the life He has called us to.

> *But we all, with open face beholding as in a glass the glory of the Lord, are changed into the same image from glory to glory, even as by the Spirit of the Lord. (2 Corinthians 3:18)*

Both men and women were formed after God's image. Genesis 1:27 says, "So God created man in his own image, in the image of God created he him; male and female created he them." He didn't give one gender more of Himself than the other. They are equally formed in God's image. Both have their place in the purpose and plans of God. Neither is superior.

And God blessed them, and God said unto them, Be fruitful, and multiply, and replenish the earth, and subdue it: and have dominion over the fish of the sea, and over the fowl of the air, and over every living thing that moveth upon the earth. (Genesis 1:28)

Both male and female were made by God, and He endowed them both with blessings. He gave each a command to carry out amazing things on earth. Both have the same commandment: To multiply and have dominion.

God is no respecter of persons (Acts 10:34; Romans 2:11). Male and female are one in Christ. Yet each is unique, and that uniqueness is not to be tampered with. A conductor orchestrates different instruments to produce a harmonious, unified sound. Together we produce a sound of harmony that expresses the multifaceted character of God.[1] We begin playing that harmony when we submit to God as co-creators.

The first step in becoming the co-creator God meant you to be is being restored.

God made a helpmate for Adam. The Hebrew word *eze* means "helper,"[2] as in someone who helps bring about something new. *Azar* means "to surround; i.e., protect or aid."[3] By looking at these words we can see that Eve was created to assist by protecting and surrounding Adam.

Eve was created from Adam's rib, symbolizing a new beginning. "And Adam said, This is now bone of my bones, and flesh of my flesh: she shall be called Woman, because she was taken out of Man" (Genesis 2:23). She came from his bone, but he was made from dirt.

They were also created in different locations. Adam was created in Eden (Genesis 2:22), but Eve was created in the garden of Eden, which was planted after Adam was created (Genesis 2:7–8). Satan was also created in the garden of Eden (Ezekiel 28:13). Satan wanted the woman to lose her place because she took his place. That's why he came to her.

Woman of God, you are a co-creator. And just like there is enmity between Satan and God, there is enmity between you and Satan. God stated in Genesis 3:15 that He would put enmity between Eve and Satan and between her seed and Satan's seed. For Eve's offspring birthed the one who would redeem humankind, and Satan births all who destroy.

Eve is a life-giver. Genesis 3:20 calls Eve, "the mother of all the living." She is also Adam's helper according to Genesis 2:18. All women mirror their Creator. You are the lifeline that allows God's blood to flow, giving life to all it is attached to.

To become the helper God needs you to be, find out what gifts He has given you to fulfill His purpose for you on the earth. There is a treasure within you that He has endowed you with. You find it all by knowing the Giver which is the Creator of all. To search for Him means you surrender all. You sacrifice time and open up your heart.

Be strong and fight so that you can become the co-creator you truly are in Him. For you were created as a co-creator, but the enemy lies to you through the circumstance of life. Stand firm in the faith and fight by casting down every lie.

Become the True Eve

To become the helper God has created you to be, with the dominion and authority He has given you, learn to exercise the right He has given you as an heir of His Kingdom. Take back what the enemy has stolen from you: your rightful place in the mountain of God.

In God's creation, nothing is a coincidence. Woman was made from bone for a reason.

The functions of bone include:

- Structural support for the mechanical action of soft tissues, such as the contraction

of muscles and the expansion of lungs
- Protection of soft organs and tissues, such as the skull
- Provision of a protective site for specialized tissues, such as the blood-forming system (bone marrow)
- A mineral reservoir whereby the endocrine system regulates the level of calcium and phosphate in the circulating body fluids.[4]

Like bone, the function of a woman is to support, to protect, and to provide.

The Hebrew word for "esteem," *eh'tsem*, can mean "bone, body, life, or strength."[5] It comes from the word *atsma,aw-stsam* means "to bind fast"[6] or "to make powerful or numerous. It also means great, and mightier."[7]

Bone is symbolic of strength, might, binding together, and power to multiply. Women carry a supernatural strength to bind things together and to multiply the Kingdom of God. There is power in a woman when she partners with the Great Craftsman.

"Ounce for ounce, our bones are stronger than steel."[8]

"Human bones, pound for pound, are four times stronger than concrete."[9]

"A cubic inch of bone can in principle bear a load of about 19,000 lbs. (8,618 kg) or more—roughly the weight of five standard pickup trucks."[10]

"Your bones get fractured due to speed and weight added in the accident."[11]

I believe God made the woman from the man's bone to let her know that He created her with a unique strength that helps her hold things together. Her strength is birthed not only in the natural but the spiritual. The enemy comes with speed and force, throwing dart after dart and weighing you down with his lies, hoping you will crack. But if you bind yourself to your Creator, nothing can stop you.

According to the articles I read, bone cells have very strong walls and a matrix that provides support to the whole skeletal system. Muscles are made from fibers, which are made from protein, and protein is made from cells. When you come into the body of Christ, you provide it with a strong wall. You build a hedge of protection around it. You bring the body shape and form, and also help the body of Christ by supporting the entire organism. Just as the body has parts that work together to bring it to its full potential, so it is with you as a member of the Kingdom of God.

You are needed and powerful. Without the strength of women, who are stronger than steel and concrete, the body of Christ is as weak as a baby.

By allowing worldly traditions and cultures to influence our thoughts regarding God's creation of women, we have failed to strengthen and empower the body of Christ. I believe that is one of the reasons most women do not walk in their full potential and power.

A woman will not easily be broken if she is hidden in the wings of her Creator. She can overcome any obstacle and make the world a better place. Strong women are heroes. They work hard and they make a difference. They don't give up.

Our bones are made for movement, and without movement, there is no life. Women are meant for movement, and without women there is no life. When women act as the bone in the body of Christ, she brings movement, and life comes into the body.

Eve came out of Adam's side. When Jesus's side was pierced on the cross, the Church was born. You are the bride of Christ. When you come to Him, you become one with Him. As Eve was the flesh of Adam's flesh and bone of his bone, so are you with the Spirit of Jesus Christ and His blood. You are one with Him. He is your head and your protector. As His bride, you are His helper, led by Him.

Team Up with the Holy Spirit

To experience all that God has in store for you, you collaborate with the Holy Spirit. The Spirit of God animates you. Without the Spirit of the Lord, you would just be a dry bone that doesn't move.

The Holy Spirit is both gentle and powerful. Let go of your own agenda, and allow the Spirit of God to move freely. Let the Spirit come upon you and take over by yielding to Him.

There is a difference between having the Holy Spirit *in* you and having the Holy Spirit come *upon* you. Let me give you an illustration of what I mean.

Let's say that water in this example is symbolic of the Holy Spirit, and an empty bottle represents a person. If water (Holy Spirit) is poured into the bottle (person), then the Spirit is within. Now if the bottle (person) is submerged under water such as a sea or a pool, then the water (representation of the Holy Spirit) is now upon the person.

We can't tell the Spirit of God, "I give You permission to take over" and then take the wheel ourselves. You may think the course you have in mind is better than the plan of God. But the Holy Spirit has already seen the best course.

Make the Holy Spirit your best friend. This relationship is built like any other relationship you form. Make time for Him and have love and respect. Be sensitive to His desires, and learn His dislikes and likes.

When you go to the mountain of God, the Spirit will come upon you like dew. You climb by worship and seeking truth as Sheba sought truth. It is the path of righteousness that will bring you to the place where God dwells.

The Holy Spirit will speak to you and teach you if you become like a child. Children believe everything they hear, and they do new things every day. So shall it be for you, my friend. Like a child, you will not be afraid to broaden your horizon and do new things. "Verily I say unto you, Whosoever shall not receive the kingdom of God as a little child shall in no wise enter therein" (Luke 18:17).

The Holy Spirit Is like a Mother

The Bible says, "That which is born of the flesh is flesh; and that which is born of the Spirit is spirit" (John 3:6). The Holy Spirit is God's gift to us.

He is our Helper (John 4:16), just as a woman is a helper to a man (Genesis 2:18). The Holy Spirit is a teacher and a guide (1 Corinthians 2:10; John 16:3). Likewise, women are called to teach and instruct their daughters (Titus 2:4–5).

Jesus told the disciples it was necessary for Him to go so that they could receive the gift of God: a Comforter, Advocate, Helper, and Counselor.

The Holy Spirit is the best help you could ever have. He convicts you when you're on the wrong path like a mother corrects her children when they are heading the wrong way.

Women Created in His Image

Did you know that God travails in birthing? Deuteronomy 32:18 says, "You neglected the Rock who had fathered you; you forgot the God who had given you birth" (NLT). When bringing things to life, travailing cannot be avoided. But just as a mother comforts her child, so does God comfort His children (Isaiah 66:13).

God compares Himself to a mother. He is a teacher, cuddler, and nurturer. "I taught Ephraim also to go, taking them by their arms; but they knew not that I healed them. I drew them with cords of a man, with bands of love: and I was to them as they took off the yoke on their jaws, and I laid meat unto them" (Hosea 11:3-4). In Isaiah 49:15, we read, "Can a woman forget her sucking child, that she should not have compassion on the son of her womb? Yea, they may forget, yet will I not forget thee."

Have Dominion, Subdue, and Lead

Women are called to have dominion over themselves and everything around them, leading out into society. God has already given you supremacy. You just need to learn to operate in it.

The word *dominion* can mean "control or authority over something or someone, political power, empire, kingdom, or reign" (KJV Dictionary). You are called to reign, so don't let the situations rule over you.

Debora had dominion over the people of Israel. May the Lord give you the Deborah anointing to have jurisdiction over the territory of your life. Use this power to shape beliefs.

To *subdue* means "to conquer, defeat, to overcome persuasion, and or to overpower and destroy the force problem"(KJV Dictionary). You are made to conquer circumstances in your life, nation and country.

Jael conquered the enemy of Israel. May you

overthrow the plans of the enemy over your life. Overcome every difficulty by getting a better understanding of the power within you. Suppress the lies.

Miriam used a musical instrument to lead (Exodus 15:20). She also led the nation along with her brothers (Micah 6:4). You were called to lead by becoming a great influencer. You become a great leader by serving others and having compassion. You will lead with a vision to bring people into breakthroughs.

You can lead as God leads if you answer the call. Walk by faith and obedience, and watch how you start to have dominion over your life, subduing everything that comes against you. Lead by progressing, gaining intellectual territory, and developing in your true identity.

Woman Are Birth Givers

Women give birth to people who can change history and enhance our world. They are also birth givers in the spirit realm as they birth the move of the Creator. Women are great intercessors who birth that of the spirit, which then manifests in the natural.

"Thus saith the Lord of hosts, Consider ye, and call for the mourning women, that they may come; and send for cunning women, that they may come: And let them make haste, and take up a wailing for us, that our eyes may run down with tears, and our eyelids gush out with waters" (Jeremiah 9:17–18). Notice how God calls women cunning. And He calls them to help. Skillful women can come against wickedness. We have a position to occupy in this war of the Kingdom of light versus the Kingdom of darkness.

Woman Stamped by God

Women have the stamp of God's image interwoven in their very being. You are part of a glorious painting showing His great craftsmanship.

To reflect His image, dig deep within you, for He has placed within you dreams that will reveal His purpose.

Saul was anointed to be king. When Samuel the prophet came to him, he told him, "Tomorrow I will let thee go, and will tell thee all that is in thine heart" (1 Samuel 9:19). Saul was not aware of what was in his heart. God used Samuel to reveal to him how he had fallen short. And yet, he would become king by God's choice. God then used other prophets to make Saul a new man. He wanted Saul to come into His image interwoven within him.

God will reveal things to you that will change your perspective about who you are. Then you can be changed into who you are destined to become. Remember that it all happens in the process. But when you know you have been stamped by God, you will see the faithfulness of God.

Samuel told David what he would become (1 Samuel 16:1-13). Yet David still had to go through a process. Samuel anointed David as King but David did not become King right away (2 Samuel 5:4). David was just a young boy when God revealed who he would become. The Bible gives us clues of this. It states that he was the youngest of eight boys.

Also, when Goliath was taunting the army of Israel, David offered to fight the giant, but Saul said he was only a boy (1 Samuel 17:33). David then came to serve King Saul, knowing one day he would replace him as king. Not only did he serve Saul, but he remained loyal to him even as King Saul looked to kill him. David went through a long process, but the revelation given to him changed him into who God said he would become.

God showed Joseph what would become of him through a dream (Genesis 37:5). He also went through a process, from the pit to slavery and from slavery to prison. Yet favor followed him, and he became that which God revealed. You will come into your destiny by the fullness of maturation and trial. When you learn that the image of God is interwoven in you, you will go from philosophy to reality.

The angels know who you are. The devil knows who you are. God wants you to know who you are. He made you, and He has a plan for you. Learn who you truly are by looking at what God says about you. Meditate on it until you start to believe it.

God will put back together all that the enemy has broken. He will reveal that which He has placed in you and restore that which you have lost.

Declaration

I will not look outside of myself but inside myself for the solution. "You, dear children, are from God and have overcome them, because the one who is in you is greater than the one who is in the world" (1 John 4:4).

CHAPTER THREE

IDENTITY FORTIFIED

Therefore if any man be in Christ, he is a new creature: old things are passed away; behold, all things are become new. (2 Corinthians 5:17)

ALL OF US have identity issues. Due to the fall of man and sin entering the world, our identity has been lost. Most people identify with their mistakes—what they've done and haven't done—and what people say about them. But in Christ our identity is redefined. He reconnects us to our God-organic identity that lies deep within us.

Have you ever let someone else define who you are? What you can and cannot do? What you should be doing? Have you nurtured lies and erected barriers within yourself? I believe we all have. That's why it's important for us to know who we are in Christ. So we can break out of the status quo, and enter into the realm of abundance that God has made available for us through His precious Son, Jesus Christ.

The world has influenced our dreams, causing us to be bound to lies that prevent us from achieving our purpose and reaching our destiny.

Shards of Glass

Our identity has been shattered into pieces. We need God's help. Our souls long to know what we were created for. We want our identity to be revealed.

Before I had my encounter with God, I saw myself as an outsider in my own family. I felt like a failure. I identified with the Ugly Duckling: unappealing and undesirable. Without a voice or a choice. Whenever I took one step forward, I took three steps back.

I thought I knew who I was. I thought I knew what love was. I thought my tragic situation was meant to be. I was lost, feeling I had no value. I tried to pull myself together. But I was not made whole until I gave it all to Him.

Now I live in my God-given identity, and I'm still learning and growing. What happened to bring about this dramatic change was that I was tired of the life I was living. I was going from one broken abusive relationship to the next. Infidelity was a cycle that told me something had to be wrong with me. Feeling like I would never be sufficient or good enough. I lost my self and worth. Finally, I gave it all to God by surrendering.

No one is perfect. "For all have sinned, and come short of the glory of God" (Romans 3:23). His redemption has nothing to do with anything we do but everything to do with Him. If you choose to rely on Him, He will show you who you are.

The Great Craftsman

Only the Great Craftsman can put the broken pieces of your life back together.

What happened in your life that caused the shards of glass in your soul? Identify your brokenness. You cannot break free from your limitations if you continue to hide behind the pain.

As a girl who grew up without her father, I began to look for love and acceptance in all the wrong places. In my first relationship as a young lady, it began with infidelity and continued with verbal and physical abuse as I got involved with others. I became a single mother of three beautiful children, and I had to support them in every way. I became a woman who felt like all odds were against me. Men put me down, using me for their own needs and pleasure, while I gave my one hundred percent to the relationship. My own family viewed me as the black sheep of the family, so I began to identify with that. Everything always seemed to go so wrong and left me feeling empty inside.

The last man who came into my life was my breaking point. Here I was, hoping for something different, just to find out it was all a lie. He was heavily on drugs, which caused him to act out, lived off of me, and brought other women to my home while I worked. I wanted to let go of him and seemed to find no way out. I would look up at the sky and tell myself there has to be more than this for me. This can not be all there is to my life.

Finally, on my birthday, we went out and everything went wrong. We got into a horrible fight. I was left in the middle of a desert not knowing where I was. Thankfully, a friend found me and guided me back home. But it didn't end there. He showed up to my house to try to mend things, and at this point I just wanted it all to be over. That same day, the woman he had been bringing into my house decided to let me know what had been going on between them, and that was when I broke.

I couldn't carry the burden on my own or live in my own way. When I'd had enough of the brokenness and wanted to be done with it, I cried into my pillow, "God, please take this pain from me. I cannot deal with it anymore. I have no more strength." He heard my cry and came swiftly. He began to work the instant I cried out.

When I cried out, God began to use people I worked with to speak into my life by prophesying. The Lord placed in my heart to move back with my mother, which I truly did not want to do. I had lived on my own from a young age. I struggled with that thought until I went to visit my mother one evening and she said, "I feel like you are supposed to move back in with us." I felt the confirmation and moved in with her quickly.

Moving in with my parents forced the man I was with to leave me alone. And within weeks, God began to pour out His love for me through His amazing people. He gave me dreams and spoke to my heart. My life completely changed.

I knew He was the only one who could take me out of the depths of darkness. He'd just been waiting for me. My will kept me in my brokenness until I finally gave in to His will. He is still working with me to remove things that I still havent let go of. It is a process of growth and we will not become completely whole until the coming of Jesus.

God wants to mend our souls. Even if you choose to continue on a broken path, He will never give up on you. He always leaves the door open for you.

Let Him In

Let God into your broken areas so that He can put all the pieces back into their rightful place. Your identity cannot be reassembled by you or any man or woman. Allow God to enter that place in your being where you are lost and hurt, that place where you hide because you're scared. Open up your heart today and tell the Lord you are ready for Him to begin creating His masterpiece within you.

Don't let pride stop you. If I would have let my pride win, I'd always take care of myself. I would not have moved back in with my parents. The situation would have not changed in the way it did. I decided to humble myself to do what I really did not want to do in order to get out of the cycle I found myself in. Pride works as a barrier that stops you from becoming all God has called you to be.

Humble yourself so that you will be able to

flourish. I decided to humble myself and move back under my parents' roof, going by their rules even though I felt like I was a grown woman and should be able to do as I wanted. Humbling myself caused me to flourish in character and in my God-given assignment. The fruit that came from humility was favor, honor and wisdom.

God will show you things inside yourself that you didn't know were there to help you mature and excel. I thought I was free, but recently through a service, He told me to let go of my pain and disappointment in men. He was no man to fail me. I thought I had already given Him all my pain, but He saw in me what I did not. There was pain that still had a hold on me. The Bible says, "The heart is deceitful above all things (Jeremiah 17:9). "Every way of a man is right in his own eyes: but the Lord pondereth the hearts" (Proverbs 21:2).

You may think your life is beyond repair, but your flaws are what make you special. Your life will tell a story that's unique to you. Whoever gets the honor of knowing you will be blessed and changed. Almighty God can restore your identity.

Metamorphosis

Everything that has been imposed on us is putting a halt to our metamorphosis. The rejection, abandonment, loss of loved ones, sickness, financial crisis, relationship failure, depression, and trauma numbs us. All this pain can stop us from growing into our full potential, and it discontinues the process of our transformation. The enemy would want nothing more than for us to stay in our brokenness so that we do not convert our nature into something incompatible.

Nothing breaks God's heart more than brokenness. The brokenness of His people breaks His heart. "The Lord is nigh unto them that are of a broken heart; and saveth such as be of a contrite spirit (Psalms 34:18). He draws near to those who are oppressed, have broken hearts, broken purpose in life due to the sufferings of this life, and to those whose spirits are in pieces. God cares about you and your future.

God has a soul (refer back to chapter one for scripture). He gets sad, angry, and happy. He has a will and emotions.

The soul of God is His heart and will. The soul of man is also the heart and will, which requires atonement. When sin entered in through Adam, it separated all of us from the heart and will of God. We all come into the world with a sinful nature, which causes separation from Him, so Jesus's blood was the atonement that paid the price for all of sin, once and for all.

If we don't look at the atonement of Christ, we will view our lives through broken glasses. When we come into the salvation of Jesus, we are restored to the Father. Now the Father can begin to bring revelation to us that opens our eyes to see what He sees in us, which is His beloved Son. He also shows us who He has made us to be. We can change the scope we are looking through. Exchange the broken glasses, and look through the lens called the love of the Father.

Brokenness can result from a broken spirit, a broken mind, or broken emotions. It comes from the result of sin—our own or someone else's. Sin breaks our relationship with God and with others. It also damages our own sense of self-worth and causes us to doubt His love for us. As a result, we can become withdrawn and resentful, which only deepens the breach in us and Him. Everyone experiences brokenness at some point in their lives.

Brokenness can lead to sin and temptation. When brokenness takes over, it's hard to get out of the wreckage.

Brokenness can lead us down many roads that God does not want us to go down. We tell ourselves we can't live the way we are living and feeling the way we do. *I'm alone. No one understands me. Why is this happening to me?* Remember, the battle isn't over. "For we wrestle not against flesh and blood, but against principalities, against powers, against the rulers of the darkness of this world, against spiritual wickedness in high places" (Ephesians 6:12).

A traumatic experience can shatter your soul and form an anxious and fearful mental attitude. Brokenness will control you unless you do something about it. Surrender the brokenness to God, and He will use it for His glory. Die to your sin, come alive in Christ, and take hold of His unchangeable and unfailing promises. They cannot be broken. "Many are the afflictions of the righteous: but the Lord delivereth him out of them all" (Psalm 34:19).

Are you prepared to use your faith in God to combat the brokenness that has kept you prisoner of all the negative thoughts and emotions?

The Scriptures declare that what the adversary intended for evil, God will make a means of good (Genesis 50:20). What the enemy meant for your harm, God will use to bring restoration and healing to you. You have been brought out of darkness into light through Jesus Christ (Colossians 1: 13). You have a reason to live, and that is Jesus Christ.

In John 10:10 Jesus said, "The thief cometh not, but for to steal, and to kill, and to destroy: I am come that they might have life, and that they might have it more abundantly." The enemy of your soul tells lies.

As anyone who has been the victim of a crime knows, the lasting impact can be much more than just the loss of material possessions. In fact, the trauma of being victimized can have a profound effect on every aspect of a person's life. Victims of theft often suffer from anxiety, insomnia, and depression. The thief not only takes what doesn't belong to them, but also robs the victim of their peace of mind. Jesus came to give us life, and not just any life, but a life that is abundant and full. In Him, we find hope and healing for the pain that has been inflicted on us.

We are molded by our past experiences. However, while we dwell in this sinful world, we are not of it (John 17: 16-26). We operate from a different dimension and live by different principles. We are from a heavenly Kingdom which does not operate as the world.

A believer lives in a dimension that is guided by principles such as love, faith, hope and charity. The world, on the other hand, is governed by different principles. These principles include greed, envy, lust, and pride. The world is also a place where people are judged by their looks and their possessions. A believer, on the other hand, is not judged by these things. Instead, they are judged by their character and their actions. As a result, a believer lives in a dimension that is higher than the world. And they are able to live happier and more fulfilling lives.

We are seated in heavenly places (Ephesians 2:6). The same Spirit that raised Jesus from the dead is in us (Romans 8:11). We can live in abundance by learning how to tap into the dimension of the Kingdom of Heaven, where there is copiousness of everything we could ever need and want.

In order to tap into this dimension, we need to learn how to open our minds and hearts to receive all that is available to us. You can enter this dimension by raising your frequency through meditation, prayer, and worshiping. When you grasp this practice, you will experience the abundance that takes many forms, including love, joy, peace, and material possessions. Once we identify the issue, a solution can be applied.

Brokenness can lead to addictions, suicide, self-harm, and even murder. Brokenness causes a person to lose control of their thoughts and actions, leading to negative consequences. However, there is hope for those who are broken. Jesus Christ is the ultimate solution to brokenness. He was Himself broken for our sake, and He offers us the chance to be made whole again. Through His death and resurrection, He conquered sin and death, making it possible for us to have eternal life.

Brokenness usually happens as a result of a lack of love. If we are broken, we can't love the way God wants us to. As broken people, we cannot show love.

Brokenness is a reflection of a broken spirit and a broken mind, and it affects all aspects of our lives, leaving us feeling lost and alone. The good news is that Jesus came to seek and save the brokenhearted. He offers us hope and healing for our brokenness. When we surrender our lives to Him, He gives us a new spirit, a new mind, and new emotions. We are no longer defined by our sin or our mistakes. We are children of God, created in His image.

Brokenness can either make you or break you, but no matter how damaged you are, there is a new day coming. You have a bright future ahead, so don't give up. Hold on to the truth of God. Life can be hard. We all go through tough times and come out the other side feeling broken. But it's important to remember that broken doesn't mean worthless. In fact, brokenness can actually be a strength. It can make you more compassionate, more empathetic, and more able to relate to others who are going through tough times of their own. With hard work and determination, you will be able to achieve anything you set your mind to.

Life can be full of surprises. Just when you think you have everything figured out, something comes along to throw you off course. I've encountered plenty of potholes and bumps along the road. I have to remind myself daily that I cannot accomplish anything on my own. But He will guide me through whatever challenges come my way as long as I stay with Him.

When you go through tough times and carry the weight of the world on your shoulders, it becomes easy to feel like you're all alone. You may think that no one understands what you're going through or that nobody cares. But the truth is, God is always with you, even in your darkest hour. He knows what you're going through and He will never leave your side. So when life gets tough, remember that you are not alone and that God is always with you.

As God brings you back to your true identity,

He will continue to reveal to you who you are. Every day you can walk in confidence, knowing that it has nothing to do with your past, your present situation, and painful circumstance, but everything to do with the One who has called you. Know who you are in Him.

As you begin to walk in your true identity, you may find that there are aspects of your life that no longer fit who you are. This is to be expected, and it is nothing to be concerned about. As you grow into your new identity, you will naturally outgrow old things. This process can be unsettling at first, but it is ultimately very freeing. As you become more comfortable with who you are, you will also become more confident. You will no longer feel the need to conform to other people's expectations or standards. Instead, you will be free to be yourself. And as you embrace your true identity, you will find that you are able to enjoy your life more fully than ever before.

Who Am I?

Jesus was the seed that died and fell into the deepest parts of the earth so that He might gather a great harvest of souls. You are the person He came for. He gave His splendor and majesty away so that you might have it all. The King made Himself a servant so that you might be a partaker of the Kingdom of Heaven. He came to restore that which was lost.

And we know that all things work together for good to them that love God, to them who are the called according to his purpose. For whom he did foreknow, he also did predestinate to be conformed to the image of his Son, that he might be the firstborn among many brethren. Moreover whom he did predestinate, them he also called: and whom he called, them he also justified: and whom he justified, them he also glorified. What shall we then say to these things? If God be for us, who can be against us? He that spared not his own Son, but delivered him up for us all, how shall he not with him also freely give us all things? Who shall lay any thing to the charge of God's elect? It is God that justifieth. Who is he that condemneth?It is Christ that died, yea rather, that is risen again, who is even at the right hand of God, who also maketh intercession for us. Who shall separate us from the love of Christ? shall tribulation, or distress, or persecution, or famine, or nakedness, or peril, or sword? As it is written, For thy sake we are killed all

the day long; we are accounted as sheep for
the slaughter. Nay, in all these things we are
more than conquerors through him that loved
us. For I am persuaded, that neither death,
nor life, nor angels, nor principalities, nor
powers, nor things present, nor things to come.
(Romans 8:28–38)

Jesus's love for you passes all understanding. He knew you and destined you from the start (Ephesians 1:4). He has called you, and He has proven your justification by offering His priceless blood on the cross.

God loved you so much that He gave His one and only Son (John 3:16) so that you could receive your heavenly inheritance. "God is holy and perfect" (1 Samuel 2:2); "He cannot dwell where sin is" (Proverbs 6:16-19).

We are all born sinners into a world filled with sin. When we accept Jesus Christ as Lord and Savior, our spirits awaken and the righteousness of Jesus covers our sins. For Christians, accepting Jesus Christ as Lord and Savior is the most important decision they will ever make. In doing so, they are acknowledging that He is the Son of God and the only path to salvation. This decision represents a radical departure from their old life, and it means committing to living according to His teachings. It is a lifelong journey that requires much effort and sacrifice, but it is also immensely rewarding. Those who accept Jesus Christ as their Lord and Savior can expect to experience His love, grace, and mercy every day. They will also find strength in Him during times of hardship and trial. Ultimately, accepting Jesus Christ as Lord and Savior is a decision that changes everything.

Every day, Jesus intercedes with God the Father for you. He understands your entire story, from your mother's womb until your last breath. You are not your background, or where you went to school, or who you grew up with, or the clothes society says you have to wear.

Shame tells you that something is wrong with you. Guilt advises you that you've done something wrong. When the Holy Spirit begins to work with you, He will redefine and demonstrate to you who you truly are. You are the offspring of God.

Every person is uniquely made and crafted by the Creator. Psalm 139:14-16 says, "I praise you, for I am fearfully and wonderfully made. Wonderful are your works; my soul knows it very well. My frame was not hidden from you, when I was being made in secret, intricately woven in the depths of the earth. Your eyes saw my unformed substance; in your book were written, every one of them, the days that were formed for me, when as yet there was none of them." We are the workmanship of the Almighty God. "The one who was and is and is to come" (Revelation 1:8) The One who knows everything.

He created you for His perfect will and purpose. Romans 9:21 says, "Does not the potter have the right to make out of the same lump of clay some pottery for special purposes and some for common use?" We are His vessels, to be used by Him.

He has placed within you a potential you may not have discovered. This fullness is reachable for you in Christ. According to 2 Corinthians 3:2–3, you are a letter. Whether you're a leader, a comforter, a healer, an inventor, an author, a warrior, a peacemaker, a worshiper, an intercessor, or a history changer, your days have been numbered by the One who created you.

Luke 12:7 says, "But even the very hairs of your head are all numbered. Fear not therefore: ye are of more value than many sparrows." You have so much to offer and so much to explore.

You are part of the chosen generation (1 Peter

2:5), born for such a time as this (Esther 4:14). A royal priesthood, a people of His possession, that you may proclaim the excellencies of Him who called you out of darkness and into His marvelous light (1 Peter 2:9). You are distinctive, unusual, and special.

Use every day wisely, for every second, minute, hour, week, month, and year is important. The world is looking for people who have fully embodied their purpose. For those who will stand up in moments of chaos. It might be you! Don't run or hide from what God has sent you to do.

It was only a few years ago that I was living in complete chaos. I didn't use my time wisely at all. I would spend hours upon hours worrying about things that, in the end, didn't matter. Or I would hide behind my fears and insecurities instead of stepping into what God had called me to do.

But that has changed. I realized that if I wanted to make a difference in this world, I needed to start using my time wisely. Each second, minute, hour, week, month, and year is important. And so I began my journey of using every day to its fullest potential. It is the reason I am here writing this book. As God placed it in my heart to do it, I began to use the time He has given me to fulfill my assignment. In the midst of chaos in the world, I am standing up to tell you that there is hope for you no matter how dark it is, because God has created you with purpose.

Ask the Holy Spirit to illuminate your purpose and destiny so that you may discover what you were created to accomplish. His assignment will bring you great pleasure. When you see the world through God's eyes, it's easy to identify who you are and why you're here. Take some time for yourself at least once a week to allow yourself to meditate on what God is telling you.

God wants you to be healed of your brokenness. Sit down with the Holy Spirit and recognize the source of your suffering. He will peel back the layers and pick up the broken pieces. He will use what looks ruined to make His masterpiece out of you. When He puts it all together, you'll be amazed at how everything is positioned in just the right spot. You'll gleam with brilliant hues you've never seen before. You are part of the scepter He holds, the light that glimmers from it. He will present it gladly for the world to see.

You can't just smile and pretend everything is fine if you want to break out, break forth, and break through. No one can deny that life is tough. No matter who you are or where you come from, you will face difficulties and hardships. At times, it can feel like the weight of the world is bearing down on you. But in the midst of all this darkness, there is still hope. There is always something to be grateful for, even on the toughest of days. And when you finally find that ray of hope, don't be afraid to grab onto it and let it lift you up.

Find your worth in Him, and let Him breathe new life into you. There is so much more waiting for you on the other side of this brokenness.

When you understand that your identity is in Jesus Christ, your mindset will begin to shift. When you come to know who you are in Christ, it will change the way you think about yourself. You will no longer see yourself as a sinner in need of constant forgiveness, but rather as a beloved child of God with a new identity. This new identity has been made possible through Christ's sacrificial death on the cross. When you understand the gravity of what He has done for you, it will change the way you see yourself and the world around you. You will begin to view yourself and others through the lens of God's grace and love. This shift in mindset will transform your life and relationships. It will also impact the way you live out your faith. As you begin to see yourself as God sees you, you will be empowered.

Remember that the damage that has been done to you can either break you or build you, depending on how you choose to carry yourself into tomorrow. In order to succeed and achieve your goals, it is important to carry yourself in a way that will help you build instead of break.

There are many different strategies and approaches that you can take to ensure that you advance and grow, rather than stumble or fall. Some key ways to maintain forward momentum include staying positive, forming strong relationships, setting clear goals and expectations, and taking actionable steps towards your objectives. Whether you are working on improving your professional career, building strong personal relationships, or simply setting out on a new journey, carrying yourself confidently will help you reach your goals and achieve success. By leaning into the future with confidence and determination, you can feel empowered as you step boldly into tomorrow. And by focusing on creating rather than eliminating, you can build yourself up while avoiding the pitfalls of self-doubt and negativity. So go forth into the world with purpose, strength, and resolve. With drive, determination, and effort, there is no limit to what you can accomplish!

There are things in life that have happened to

you that weren't your fault. All the negative things people in your life have said about you have brought you down and made you doubt yourself. That doesn't matter. I know that when people say things to you or about you, it can be very painful, but remember that only what God says about you is what truly matters. When you begin to walk in your true identity in Christ, others' negative opinions will no longer have the same effect on you. People will always talk, so don't focus on what they have said. Instead, put your attention on what you want to achieve. Don't let anyone else's opinion of you hold you back. What matters is how you see yourself, because if you believe in yourself, you can achieve anything.

Don't continue to be broken by the enemy. One of the greatest struggles we all face is learning to let go of the past and move on with our lives. So often, we are battered and broken by the trials and tribulations of this world, filled with pain, sorrow, and struggle. And it feels like we simply cannot prevail against these hardships – that we are destined to be defeated by them time and time again. But that is not true! We can fight back against our enemies – those hurtful memories, crushing setbacks, and deep-seated wounds. With faith in ourselves and in a higher power, we can rise above our pasts and claim victory over every challenge that confronts us. Don't allow yourself to continue to be broken by the enemy— fight back, take control of your life, and step into your destiny with power, confidence, and hope! You have everything you need within you; let nothing hold you back from unleashing your full potential. So turn fear into courage, and let your light shine on this dark world. You were created for greatness. Don't waste another moment living beneath its shadows! Instead, claim what rightfully belongs to you—a life full of opportunity, joy, beauty, strength, love—a glorious existence better than you ever imagined.

The devil has sown seeds of doubt in your mind. The enemy loves to take advantage of our weakness. He wants you to doubt yourself and your abilities, but you cannot let him win. Now is the time to do something about it by stepping out in faith. It's time to stand up and declare that you are a child of God, and you will not be shaken by doubt. Remember whose you are and whose truth you are supposed to believe. Fight for your faith by stepping out in faith, believing He will do what He promises.

The mind is a powerful weapon if we know how to use it. It can be used to overcome obstacles, achieve goals, and create success. However, in order to use the mind effectively, we must first learn how to harness its power. One way to do this is through visualization. By picturing ourselves achieving our goals, we can program our minds for success. Additionally, it is important to focus on positive thoughts and affirmations. These positive statements help to reprogram the subconscious mind and increase our belief in ourselves. When we combine visualization with positive thinking, we create a powerful tool that can help us achieve any goal. With the right mindset, anything is possible.

Your body contains a spirit that includes consciousness and thinking. Every cell in your body is informed by your thoughts. Memories are stored in your body of things you've heard, seen, and experienced. Your mind needs renewal to change your thought patterns so that it can store new memories to fortify your identity.

Let your mind dwell on the goodness of life. You are surrounded by beauty and opportunity every day. Take time to appreciate it.

The way you react to your circumstances is a sign of what has taken root in your mind. Our circumstances are a reflection of what is going on inside of us. If we react to our circumstances in a negative way, it is a sign that we have allowed negative thoughts and emotions to take root in our minds. On the other hand, if we react to our circumstances in a positive way, it is a sign that we have allowed positive thoughts and emotions to take root in our minds.

If your mind is rooted in fear, anxiety and insecurity, then that is what will be reflected in your actions and reactions. However, if your mind is rooted in love, faith and trust, then you will act out of those virtues. Your thoughts become things, so choose wisely what you allow to take root in your mind. You are not a victim of circumstance; you are the creator of your life through your thoughts, emotions and actions. Choose to create a life that is rooted in love, joy and abundance, and watch as those things begin to blossom in your life.

Renewing your mind is a process and as you dwell on the goodness of God, it may cause a little pain or discomfort as you face your fears and hurts that do not align with the truths of God. Imagine for a moment that your mind is like a computer. Over time, it gets filled with all sorts of junk: harmful programming, outdated ideas, and negative thinking. This junk can weigh you down and prevent you from reaching your full potential. That's why it's important to renew your mind on a regular basis. Just as you regularly clean out your computer's hard drive, you need to periodically clean out your mind. This process may cause a little pain or discomfort as you face your fears and hurts, but it's essential for living a healthy and happy life. By renewing your mind, you'll be able to let go of the past and move forward into the future with hope and confidence.

By reconstructing your mind through the renewing power of the Word of God, you will become whole. When we allow ourselves to be transformed by the renewing power of God's Word, we experience a sense of inner wholeness and completeness that is impossible to achieve through any other means. This transformation begins at the deepest level of our being, with our mind. Through giving ourselves over to Scripture and cultivating focused thought patterns that reflect its truth, we can rewire our minds to be ever more in tune with the will and purposes of God. With practice, this process of reconstruction becomes easier and more automatic, until we begin to see all areas of our lives come into alignment with His word and will. So if you are striving for inner peace or simply want to become a more complete version of who you already are, know that your salvation comes not from good works or material wealth but from rebuilding your mind through the power of God's Word.

Prayer

Lord God, I pray that You would reveal to me the source of the devil's lies in my life. In the name of Jesus, I ask You to uncover those lies so the strong grip of brokenness will break. Take me out of perplexity and into clarity, Lord. Amen.

Declaration

No matter how broken I am, I can be transformed.

CHAPTER FOUR

RECONSTRUCT YOUR MIND

The eyes of your understanding being enlightened; that ye may know what is the hope of his calling, and what the riches of the glory of his inheritance in the saints. (Ephesians 1:18)

YOU CAN HAVE a different outcome in life by learning to renew your mind. Be attentive to your thoughts. Filter your thinking. Every day, you make hundreds of decisions that shape your thoughts, emotions, and actions. And every day, you have the opportunity to choose thoughts that will empower you to create the life you want. When you make the decision to renew your mind, you are choosing to focus on thoughts and actions that will lead you down the path of success and happiness. You are taking control of your life and making the choice to create a better future for yourself. So start today by renewing your mind, and see how quickly your life starts to change for the better.

Thinking is critical if you're going to put on the mind of Christ. Your thoughts determine your actions and your reactions. They color your perception of the world and yourself. So if you want to think like Christ, you should be intentional about your thoughts. Be willing to question assumptions and rethink your perspective. Be open to new ideas and different ways of seeing things.

To discover how the mind works and what you can do with your mind, I suggest you read Dr. Caroline Leaf's *Think, Learn, Succeed,* and listen to teachings from Cindy Trimm. You can go on Youtube to find teachings from Cindy Trimm. These are amazing resources to understanding how the mind works and great applications to living life to the fullest in God's purpose for each individual.

Three Types of Voices

In your mind, you will hear the voice of the enemy, the voice of the flesh, and the voice of God. Here are some examples on how to distinguish between the three.

The Voice of the Enemy

Satan launches missiles into your mind based on words spoken in your past, events you have experienced, and circumstances you've encountered. He often employs deception to manipulate you.

In the Garden of Eden, the idea of eating the forbidden fruit did not come from Eve. She perceived the thought as her own, but it actually came from the adversary. Satan planted it in her mind. His idea became her idea.

In Matthew 16:22–23, Jesus recognized that the words that came out of Peter's mouth were not his. The thought originated from Satan, which is why Jesus said, "Get thee behind me, Satan" (Matthew 16:23).

When you're bogged down by a negative thought or action, it's difficult to get out from under its influence. When Satan infects your mind, he can alter your behavior.

The Voice of the Flesh

Romans 8:6 says, "For to be carnally minded is death; but to be spiritually minded is life and peace." The voice of the flesh will set up false perceptions and false values in your mind, which will lead you to destruction and death. If our minds are governed by the Holy Spirit, we will have complete harmony in the soul.

Paul said, "I don't really understand myself, for I want to do what is right, but I don't do it. Instead, I do what I hate" (Romans 7:15 NLT). The flesh desires the opposite of what the Spirit of God wants.

The flesh speaks through lust and pride. Some desires of the heart may appear to be from God, but they are actually of the flesh. Jeremiah 17:9 tells us, "The heart is deceitful above all things, and desperately wicked: who can know it?" Only God can understand it.

The voice of the flesh will urge you to give in to its cravings.

The Voice of God

The voice of God will speak truth to every situation.

If you want to hear His voice, go to His Word. He speaks through Scripture.

He will also speak to your heart and mind as you worship Him. If an idea suddenly drops into your spirit while you're praising God, that is His word to you.

God can also speak to you through prophets

if they are speaking from the truth of God and the heart of God. Always measure any prophecy against the Bible to distinguish the validity of the voice.

Discerning Voices

The Greatest Craftsman can give you the power to know which voice is speaking to you. If you listen to the lies of the enemy or your own flesh, you will lose. But if you hear the voice of God and obey it, you will win. Pay close attention to discern all the noise around you and within you.

What are your thoughts saying to you? Has your mind been aligned to the authority of Jesus Christ? Have you responded in obedience?

Understanding the Brain

The brain contains the mind, which is the seat of our thoughts. The mind controls the brain.

Your brain's cognitive processes are the result of electrical and chemical signals that pass through it. The mind uses the brain to communicate between the body and the spirit. Your soul and spirit provide energy to every cell in your body. This energy creates life and consciousness.

In humans and primate species there are neurons called mirror neurons. These brain cells activate when we see someone doing something. For example, when a chimpanzee sees its mother opening a nut with a rock and then tries to imitate her with another nut. Mirror neurons are related with empathic, social and imitations behavior. They are a fundamental tool for learning.[12].

At any given moment, your brain is humming with activity. Neurons are firing, sending signals back and forth between different areas of the brain. And among all of these neurons are a special type called mirror neurons. Mirror neurons get their name from their ability to imitate the behavior of the people around us. When we see someone else doing something—whether it's yawning, laughing, or even just reaching for a cup of coffee—our mirror neurons send out a signal that allows us to "mirror" that same behavior. In this way, mirror neurons play an important role in social interaction and communication. But they don't just stop at imitation; they also help us to understand the emotions and intentions of others. In other words, mirror neurons allow us to feel empathy for others. So next time you see someone yawning, remember that it's not just contagious. It's also a result of your brain's natural ability to connect with others.

A thought can also be created individually. We have the ability to create thoughts through our imagination. However, many people don't understand how to control this power. When you hear the word "thought," what comes to mind? For some people, thoughts are just words that appear in their head. But thoughts are much more than that. Thoughts are also feelings, images, and memories. And just like we can have different types of thoughts, we can also have different ways of thinking. Some people might think mostly in words, while others might think mostly in pictures. Some people might think mainly about the present, while others might spend more time thinking about the past or the future. And some people might have very negative thoughts, while others might have very positive thoughts. So as you can see, thoughts are not just random words that appear in our head. Thoughts are complex and varied, and we all have our own individual way of thinking. Many people don't realize that they have the power to control their thoughts. Just like we can choose what to say out loud, we can also choose what to think in our head. If you find yourself thinking negative thoughts, try to focus on something positive instead. Or if you find yourself dwelling on the past, try to focus on the present moment. It might take some practice, but it is possible to control your thoughts. And once you learn how to control your thoughts, you'll be surprised at how much power you have over your own life. So the next time you find yourself thinking negative thoughts, remember that you have the power to change them. Choose to focus on something positive instead, and see how your life changes for the better.

When we're young, we absorb energy from those around us. As we mature, we become more aware of our own thoughts and feelings. Then we can think, feel, and act independently. But throughout our lives, our brains are constantly looking for similarities in behavior between others and ourselves. We can imitate someone or something and learn from them.

If we live in the Word of God, we can begin to imitate it. If we surround ourselves with godly people, we can grow spiritually.

You can observe the effect your thoughts have on others through their behavior, especially those who are around you a lot. When you're in a good mood, the people you're with will become happier. If you are negative, those around you will also be unhappy. You can affect the people around you by changing your own mood.

Your thoughts are powerful because they control what happens in your life and the lives of everyone around you.

Stay aware of where you are picking up thoughts. Social media affects the way millions of people live and feel. It alters the way people think. If you spend less time on social media and more time with the Greatest Craftsman, He will craft your mind into His.

Free your mind by learning to control your thoughts, and you will unleash a world of possibilities. To alter your world and your destiny, just change the way you think.

"For as he thinketh in his heart, so is he" (Proverbs 23:7). Wherever your thoughts dwell is where your energy goes, and energy has power. If you do what you've always done, you'll receive what you've always received. Partner with the Holy Spirit, and you can cast every mountain into the sea (Mark 11:23). Cast out every thought that keeps you captive. Often, it is our own thoughts that hold us back and keep us from achieving our full potential. We may believe that we are not good enough, or that we do not deserve success. These negative thoughts can become like a prison, holding us captive and preventing us from moving forward. If we want to break free, we need to cast out these thoughts and replace them with positive ones.

The mind is a strong tool. It is your weapon. When used correctly, it can be a powerful weapon against stress, anxiety, and depression. It can also be used to improve our memory and concentration, and to increase our overall well-being. With a little effort, anyone can learn how to harness the power of the mind and use it to their advantage. So fix your mind on Christ. Read God's Word, and focus on Jesus's finished work. "Think about the things of heaven, not the things of earth" (Colossians 3:2 NLT).

Joshua 1:8 states, "This book of the law shall not depart out of thy mouth; but thou shalt meditate therein day and night, that thou mayest observe to do according to all that is written therein: for then thou shalt make thy way prosperous, and then thou shalt have good success."

Meditate on the Word of God, apply what you read, and you will flourish and succeed. Scripture cannot fail. It is living and active.

"Blessed is the man that walketh not in the counsel of the ungodly, nor standeth in the way of sinners, nor sitteth in the seat of the scornful. But his delight is in the law of the Lord; and in his law doth he meditate day and night" (Psalm 1:1–2). As you continue to dwell on God's words, your mind will be molded to His. Your ideas will conform to His thoughts. And you'll live according to the life He has designed for you.

Renew your mind by the washing of the Word of God. As Christians, one of the most important things we can do is renew our minds by the washing of the Word of God. When we allow the Word to cleanse our thoughts, it purifies our hearts and minds, transforming us into the image of Christ. It also helps us to better understand God's will for our lives and gives us the wisdom and knowledge we need to live for Him. In addition, the Word equips us to resist temptation and overcome sinful habits. As we meditate on Scripture and apply its truths to our lives, we are daily being renewed in our minds and hearts, becoming more like Christ each day. Know what God says about you and settle it in your mind. Then there will be no room for mind viruses such as fear, doubt, unbelief, depression, unforgiveness, or bitterness. You will achieve more than you ever thought possible and go to destinations you never imagined. Open yourself to the reality of a joyful life in Christ, regardless of what is happening in your life.

As you learn how to think as God thinks, your mind will be reinvigorated with His Word. The

Bible states that if you fully obey the Lord your God and carefully follow all of His commands, the Lord will make you the head and not the tail; if you pay attention to the commands of the Lord your God and carefully follow them, you will always be at the top, never at the bottom (Deuteronomy 28:1, 13). You are the light of the world (Matthew 5:14–16) and the salt of the earth (Matthew 5:13). You are a force to be reckoned with.

You are the bride of Christ, and He paid a great price to obtain you. He wants to wash you with His precious blood, which will cleanse you, and His precious word, which will heal, restore, and strengthen you. If you look for Him, you will find Him.

"The light of the body is the eye: therefore when thine eye is single, thy whole body also is full of light; but when thine eye is evil, thy body also is full of darkness. Take heed therefore that the light which is in thee be not darkness. If thy whole body therefore be full of light, having no part dark, the whole shall be full of light, as when the bright shining of a candle doth give thee light." (Luke 11:34–36)

The word eye also means the mind, and here we find the conscience. According to *Vine's Complete Expository Dictionary*, one of the meanings of the word *conscience* is "co-knowledge (with one-self), the witness borne to one's conduct by conscience, that faculty by which we apprehend the will of God, as that which is designed to govern our lives."[13] Test your conscience and validate that it's in line with the Bible. Examine everything you believe, think, and do in order to see if it aligns with God's Word.

If your conscience has been renewed by the washing of the Word, you will be able to discern the thoughts God has for you. We are commanded by the Word of God to take our thoughts captive (2 Corinthians 10:5). If you let darkness filter in, confusion will stop you from walking in wholeness.

God Gave Women the Ability to Think Differently

God has endowed women with the capacity to think deeply and thoroughly. Perhaps this is why men tell us we think too much! But with our complex minds, we can multitask more easily than men. Let me show you what I mean from the studies I found:

In 2013, a study conducted at the University of Princeton and the University of Pennsylvania examined the brains of nearly a thousand men and women. The researchers were trying to figure out whether there were any notable differences in the structure of the examined male and female brains. And indeed, this is what they found:

- *Male brains are on average 8% larger than female brains. However, the neural cells of female brains show a greater number of linkages.*
- *Female brains carry a great amount of linkages between the left and the right part of the brain. A male brain on the other hand has more linkages between its front and back part. This is evidence that women are better at basing a decision on analytical (left part of the brain) as well as intuitive (right part of the brain) grounds.*
- *However, this does not apply to the cerebellum of a brain as there are more linkages between the left and the right part of the cerebellum in a male brain than in that of a female brain. This indicates that men can master complex movement sequences such as skiing more easily.*
- *The so-called limbic system on the other hand is more pronounced in the female brain. One of the things the limbic system is responsible*

for is the emotional evaluation of social and interpersonal interactions such as conversations, leading to the assumption that women are more sensitive in emotionally evaluating social interactions.[14]

God gave women the ability to think differently from men for many reasons. One reason is that women are usually the ones who have to bear children. This means that they have to be able to think and make decisions quickly in order to protect their children. Another reason is that women are often the ones who have to take care of the home and the family. This means that they need to be able to think creatively in order to solve problems. Finally, God gave women the ability to think differently because He knew that they would need it in order to survive in a world that is often hostile and dangerous. By giving them this gift, He ensured that they would always be able to find a way to safety and success.

Throughout history, women have often been seen as subordinate to men, but it is clear that God intended for them to be equals. Women tend to be more intuitive and compassionate than men, and they are often able to see the world in a different light. This difference in perspective can be a valuable asset, particularly when it comes to solving problems. In a world that is often dominated by logic and reason, the ability to think differently can be a powerful tool. It is one of the many ways that God has designed women to be unique.

However, both men and women are equally important. The way a man processes his thinking is all vitally important to a woman's life. It is also important to remember that we are all individuals with our own unique ways of thinking, and neither is superior to God. In God's eyes, both are needed. As women, we do need to remember that the man is the head of the family, and we are called to submit to the husband.

Shift Your Mindset

Romans 12:2 instructs us to renew our minds. We all have false beliefs and harmful patterns of thinking that have been ingrained in us by our families, our culture, and our society. In order to renew our minds, we need to become aware of these false beliefs and start to question them. We also should learn new, more positive ways of thinking. This can be a challenge, but it is possible with God's help.

The devil wants to take all that God intended for good. The human mind is the battlefield. The battle between good and evil is fought every day, in every person's mind. It is a battle between the desires of the flesh and the promptings of the Spirit. And it is a battle that we must all fight, if we want to avoid being controlled by sin.

The devil knows our weaknesses, and he will try to tempt us with whatever he thinks will lure us away from God. But we don't have to succumb to his schemes. We can resist him, by staying close to God and obedient to His Word. When we do, we can be confident that God will work all things together for our good (Romans 8:28). So let us not give up or grow weary in this battle. Instead, let us fix our eyes on Jesus, the Author and Perfecter of our faith (Hebrews 12:2), and trust Him to give us the victory.

The mind can have a tremendous impact on our lives in a way that can be either good or bad. The mind is a powerful thing. It can be our best ally or our worst enemy. It can help us to achieve great things or hold us back from reaching our full potential. The choice is ours. If we use our minds to focus on negative thoughts, we will likely find ourselves in a negative place. We may dwell on past failures and allow them to define us. We may become discouraged and give up on our dreams. On the other hand, if we choose to focus on positive thoughts, we can create a positive reality for ourselves. We can believe in ourselves and our abilities. We can overcome obstacles and achieve success.

The mind is powerful. 1 Corinthians 2:16 says, "For who hath known the mind of the Lord, that he may instruct him? but we have the mind of Christ." We just have to access it and enter into it. To truly understand the mind of Christ, we must first examine our own minds. Every thought and feeling we have is shaped by our individual experiences and perspectives. In order to know Christ's mind, we must be willing to let go of our own way of thinking and see the world through His eyes. This can be a challenge, but it is essential if we want to know God's will for our lives. When we pray for guidance, we need to be open to hearing what Christ has to say, even if it goes against our own ideas. Only then can we begin to understand the mind of Christ and follow His lead.

The mind generates energy through thinking, feeling, and choice. Every day, we are faced with an endless stream of choices. Some of these choices are small and insignificant, such as what to wear or what to eat. Others are more consequential, such as whether to pursue a new opportunity or stick with the status quo. But each and every choice we make has an impact on our lives, and on the world around us.

The power of choice should not be underestimated. Every time we make a choice, we are generating energy. This energy can be positive or negative, depending on the nature of the choice. Positive choices lead to positive outcomes, while negative choices can have negative consequences. The key is to be mindful of the choices we make.

Prayer

Lord God, may our minds be set free from anything that has been controlling us. We ask You to send the Holy Spirit to reveal the root of every mind virus so we can remove them and allow Your mind to be formed in us. Amen.

Declaration

I will have the mind of Christ!

CHAPTER FIVE

GENETIC CODE REBORN

For the life of the flesh is in the blood: and I have given it for you upon the altar to make atonement for your souls: for it is the blood that maketh atonement for the soul. (Leviticus 17:11)

TRAUMA CAN BE passed down from one generation to the next. Parents who have experienced trauma may pass on the harmful effects to their children, who pass it on to succeeding generations. Children in families with high levels of trauma inherit this pattern in themselves and their grandchildren.

Chromosomal DNA, which is responsible for transmitting physical traits such as hair type, eye color, and nose shape, is less than 2 percent of our total DNA. The other 98 percent is noncoding DNA (ncDNA), which is responsible for the emotional, behavioral, and personality traits we inherit. When people experience significant trauma, their ncDNA can actually change.[15] This may explain why we sometimes don't understand why we feel certain emotions.

Generational Curse

Trauma passed down to successive generations is a curse. In Exodus 20:5, God states, "I lay the sins of the parents upon their children; the entire family is affected—even children in the third generation and fourth generations of those who reject me" (NLT). Numbers 14:18 says, "The Lord is longsuffering, and of great mercy, forgiving iniquity and transgression, and by no means clearing the guilty, visiting the iniquity of the fathers upon the children unto the third and fourth generation."

Adam and Eve sinned, and because of their decisions and actions, all humankind is born into sin. The power of evil puts us in bondage until we are restored.

Curses are why many people suffer today. They feel trapped in bondage to a power that works to keep them captive. Such a stronghold keeps us from entering into the freedom made available to us through Jesus Christ.

God wants to free you, starting today. His Spirit can show you what needs to be broken off in your life and how to break it.

We have a choice: blessing or curse. Life or death. The price for our redemption was paid in full. You can break every ground the enemy has over your life. We have the power to break through any barrier that stands in our way. We can choose to be victorious, no matter what the enemy throws at us. So don't give up, don't give in. You have everything you need to win. Just keep fighting, and eventually you will break through to the other side. Break the lies that were created by your ancestors, and you will be transformed. We can choose to live our lives according to our own truths. By doing so, we can create a more authentic and fulfilling life for ourselves and future generations. It will not be easy, but it is necessary if we want to create a future that is free from the oppression of the past.

If trauma can alter your DNA, so can the love of God. Goodness and blessing will be passed down to a thousand generations. When God lavishes you with His love, that changes everything.

DNA Transformed

Romans 8:28 says, "And we know that all things work together for good to them that love God, to them who are the called according to his purpose." When we are reborn in the Spirit, everything is transformed, including our DNA.

Sin has caused trauma to be transferred to you, but you can break the covenant made by your parents or grandparents by coming into the new covenant made by the blood of Christ when you enter into the Father through salvation. He created your DNA. He wove you into your family tree. Even if it looks messed up, there is purpose in it. You may be the one who restores and redeems your family line.

Through Christ's blood we are made new, washed clean, transformed. His blood, which was shed on the cross, has given us life. It allows us to come into wholeness and freedom. His blood also gives us life and blessings on earth.

Do you want to come into that freedom? Then do it! By surrendering in all to God. Every hurt, every belief, every emotion, and every situation. He is waiting for you to break all the trauma passed down through your ancestors. It may seem impossible, but all things are possible for those who believe in Him (Mark 9:23). Let's start right now by breaking that generational trauma that has affected you for so long.

Trauma Broken

Jesus died for your sins. He also died to break the curses that have been passed down to you. "Therefore if any man be in Christ, he is a new creature: old things are passed away; behold, all things are become new" (2 Corinthians 5:17). When we are reborn in Christ, we are made whole. All things are restored in Him. You are not alone, and you are not helpless.

> *"Christ hath redeemed us from the curse of the law, being made a curse for us: for it is written, Cursed is everyone that hangeth on a tree" (Galatians 3:13).*

Here are five steps you can take to break free from trauma.

1. Gain insight into your bloodline history

Ask family members if they have experienced problems such as depression, anxiety, fear, loneliness, or anger. If your parents or their relatives have dealt with such things, it is a generational curse. If your relatives don't want to talk about it, which is common, ask the Holy Spirit to reveal it to you. In a journal, write down everything that your family members or the Holy Spirit tell you.

2. Read articles in God's constitution

Search for Scriptures that speak about the trauma you are wrestling with. Write them down as declarations. Such as:

> *"Casting all your care upon him; for he careth for you." (1 Peter 5:7)*

> *"Fear thou not; for I am with thee: be not dismayed; for I am thy God: I will strengthen thee; yea, I will help thee; yea, I will uphold thee with the right hand of my righteousness." (Isaiah 41:10)*

> *He shall cover thee with his feathers, and under his wings shalt thou trust: his truth shall be thy shield and buckler.Thou shalt not be afraid for the terror by night; nor for the arrow that flieth by day; Nor for the pestilence that walketh in darkness; nor for the destruction that wasteth at noonday. (Psalms 91:4-6)*

Take your declarations into prayer. Use them as weapons you release into the atmosphere. Go boldly into the courtroom of God to plead your case. Use these Scriptures against your accuser.

3. Enter the courtroom with repentance

Ask God for forgiveness for yourself and your family members. Ezra 9:5–6 says, "At the time of the sacrifice, I stood up from where I had sat in mourning with my clothes torn. I fell to my knees and lifted my hands to the Lord my God. I prayed" (NLT).

Pray the words of Ezra 9:6–15 over yourself. Praying God's own words is your right and freedom.

When Ezra asked God for forgiveness, he mentioned "our" sins, even though he was not in the wrong. He understood that he and the people of God were all bound to one another. In the same way, when you stand before God in His courtroom, ask for forgiveness even if you were not part of a particular fault. Ask Him to wash away the guilt from your ancestors, yourself, and your children for generations to come. Your soul is also stained along with theirs.

4. Fast

According to Isaiah 58:6, the fasting that pleases God will free the wrongly imprisoned, will lighten the burden of those who work for you, will set the oppressed free, and will remove the chains that bind.

There is no right or wrong formula for abstaining from food for a period of time. Pray about it, and God will guide you.

Through fasting, salvation will come and wounds will heal. When you fast and pray, He will hear you and come quickly.

5. Study the Bible

To get the vision of God for your life, you need to be in the Word of God. If you want to change the pattern in your DNA, visualize what God has for you. Set your gaze upon Him instead of what is around you. People who have no vision for their lives feel no purpose. But if you read the Scriptures, God will give you vision. Meditate on the Word day and night and follow its instructions. Then you will prosper in all you do.

Your epigenetics change when you meditate on the Word of God and visualize His vision, no matter what kind of trauma has come to you.

You may have experienced suffering right

from your mother's womb. If you were an unwanted child, you grew up with a sense of rejection that affected your soul and every aspect of your life. You question what's wrong with you even though the circumstances around your birth were not your fault.

People who feel lonely even while surrounded by loved ones tend to keep themselves away from others, and then depression settles in.

You may have been subjected to physical or emotional abuse. Or perhaps you're from a shattered family. Whatever your narrative is, your Creator can rewrite your story to the one written in heaven.

If you have not received Christ as your personal Savior, I encourage you to do so. He will break the curses that have been passed down to you. All you have to do is repent, which means you turn from all that has kept you away from God, and you confess and accept Jesus as your Lord and Savior. If you have received Jesus as your Savior but are still dealing with these issues, maybe you haven't allowed Him into those areas and asked Him to be Lord over them. Or you may need further deliverance. Speak with your pastor or other church leaders. If you don't have a church home, find a place where you feel surrounded by the family of God who can help you become free.

Undergoing a Process

The process of becoming whole isn't easy, but God can break you out of confinement if you trust Him to do so. Then you will see who you are in Him and what He has for you.

You are not alone. Every person on earth has gone through trials that have caused trauma. But God can turn the pain into greatness. You may not be able to see the horizon during your darkest hour. But if you trust God, you will see the light break through.

Declaration

I choose this day, a life of blessing. By the power of the blood of Christ, I will be transformed. Every curse is broken off of my bloodline. I now take on the DNA of the Holy Spirit as I enter into God.

CHAPTER SIX

The THRESHING FLOOR

But they know not the thoughts of the Lord, neither understand they his counsel: for he shall gather them as the sheaves into the floor. Arise and thresh, O daughter of Zion: for I will make thine horn iron, and I will make thy hoofs brass: and thou shalt beat in pieces many people: and I will consecrate their gain unto the Lord, and their substance unto the Lord of the whole earth (Micah 4:12–13)

ONCE YOU HAVE come up to the mountain of the Greatest Craftsman, you will be placed on His threshing floor. A threshing floor is a large, open space with a hard surface on which grain is threshed with a flail, often located on a hilltop. In the threshing process, the edible portion of grain is loosened from the straw it is bound to.

God's threshing floor is also set on a hilltop. It is a place of preparation and opportunity, of testing and trials, of growth and freedom. There are things that need to be removed from us. The threshing floor is where all gets tested, and only that which is of the Spirit remains.

God loves us too much to leave us the way we are. He wants us to grow in Him, and in order for that to happen, He must put us through this process of threshing. For we are meant to go from being a spiritual baby to a mature child of God. The good news is, He helps us through it and we are never alone.

Achieving greatness is not going to happen overnight. But you will come into greatness if you keep taking steps forward without giving up.

In 2 Samuel 24:16–25, we see the significance of the threshing floor to David. He would not allow it to just be given to him; he knew he needed to pay for it. He then built an altar on the threshing floor so the people could sacrifice and worship there.

Remember that David was a man who went through a long hard process before reaching the promises of God for his life. Him purchasing the threshing floor and knowing the value of it is very significant.

God is calling us to give the sacrifice of worship on the threshing floor to show our appreciation for Him.

We tend to appreciate something more if we've earned it than when it is given to us. If God just set us at the top without any sacrifice on our part, we would not glorify Him. We would glorify ourselves.

Solomon built the house of the Lord on the threshing floor his father David had prepared. We need to come to the threshing floor so that God can build His temple in us.

The threshing floor is where you and I decrease and God increases (John 3:30). We must empty ourselves of anything that is not of the Spirit of the Lord. Then all that remains will be those things that are true and right and pleasing to God.

When God's grace enters a situation, He turns the dark side of our existence into something wonderful. He shakes off everything that cannot stand in His presence. This is the place where we experience His amazing love.

Going through the threshing floor of the Greatest Craftsman means experiencing trials and tribulations. You will suffer. 2 Thessalonians 1:4 says, "We ourselves glory in you in the churches of God for your patience and faith in all your persecutions and tribulations that ye endure." Paul commends them for their patience and faith in difficult times.

According to *Strong's Exhaustive Concordance of the Bible, tribulation* means "a pressing, pressure."[16] This reminds me of Jesus's tribulation in the Garden of Olives, where He was so anguished that He physically sweated drops of blood.

Sometimes trials can cause us to feel like we are bleeding on the inside. As you read this chapter, I hope you will be encouraged and strengthened in your faith as you gain an understanding of why these trials happen.

The word *tribulation* comes from the Latin word *tribulum*. A tribulum is a tool used in a threshing floor to separate the grain. It is a plank of wood with sharp teeth made from steel or rocks. This tool is run over the wheat back and forth or in circles.

This is what happens when we endure tribulations. Hardships and suffering run over our lives until they separate what God wants to remove from our lives. Trials are vital for our maturity.

Threshing also separates the bad seed from the good.

Matthew 13:38–39 says, "The field is the world; the good seed is the children of the kingdom; but the tares are the children of the wicked one; the enemy that sowed them is the devil: the harvest is the end of the world; and the reapers are the angels." This refers to the final threshing process for mankind.

The trials we are going through now are for our personal benefit, to make us pleasing in the sight of God. This is better and more beneficial for us than the end-time threshing floor.

Leviticus 26:5 says, "Your threshing shall reach unto the vintage, and the vintage shall reach unto the sowing time: and ye shall eat your bread to the full, and dwell in your land safely."

Romans 5:3–5 says, "We glory in tribulations also: knowing that tribulation worketh patience; patience, experience; and experience hope: and hope maketh not ashamed; because the love of God is shed abroad in our hearts by the Holy Ghost which is given unto us." This is how character is built and how we become more like the Lord.

We Decrease So That He Can Increase

You belong to God the Father and the Lord Jesus

Christ. Jesus died to release you from the legal claims the devil had against you due to your sin. He took your place. Now you belong to Him. But you also have freedom.

Jesus was the seed that died to bring about a great harvest. We are His harvest. But we start as seeds.

When a seed is planted in the ground, it sits in darkness as the components of the soil break down the seed until its outer shell cracks open. The life inside the seed then puts forth roots and grows until it becomes a plant, which reproduces itself into many more seeds.

The darkness you face will cause your shell, your flesh, to die. It will crack under the pressure and then it will open up so that the life of Christ in you may be given unto many others.

If we are going to make an impact in this world, we must pick up our cross and follow Jesus. Mark 8:34 says, "When he had called the people unto him with his disciples also, he said unto them, Whosoever will come after me, let him deny himself, and take up his cross, and follow me." Taking the cross is a metaphor. The Romans made convicted criminals bear their crosses when they were going to the place where they would be executed. It communicated to all, "This person is already dead."

When we experience a season without tribulation, we may become complacent and stop growing in the Lord. But when we are on the threshing floor, we receive the abundance of the Kingdom. John 12:24–25 says, "Verily, verily, I say unto you, Except a corn of wheat fall into the ground and die, it abideth alone: but if it die, it bringeth forth much fruit. He that loveth his life shall lose it; and he that hateth his life in this world shall keep it unto life eternal." Before we can go up, we must first go down.

How much fruit do you want to bear with your life? The more you want, the more willing you must be to undergo distress and pressure. For only through this process will you be prepared and equipped for the harvest.

The Greatest Craftsman's Test that Humbles

James 1:2–4 says, "My brethren, count it all joy when ye fall into divers temptations; knowing this, that the trying of your faith worketh patience. But let patience have her perfect work, that ye may be perfect and entire, wanting nothing." Enduring tests will humble you. That's when you will learn to rely on the Greatest Craftsman.

"Before destruction the heart of man is haughty, and before honour is humility" (Proverbs 18:12). You cannot do anything in your own strength or your own ability. It all comes from Him, and it is all in Him.

Testing will not allow you to exalt yourself. It will ensure that you are ready to obtain what God wants to give you.

Before you can get a driving license, you must get tested to make sure you can safely operate a vehicle. Before God can trust you with His Kingdom, He must first humble you and then empower you. He needs to know whether you will please yourself, please others, or please Him.

Humility leads to confidence that God will show up.

Humility is not developed overnight. It requires patience. But it does have benefits, like being able to recognize your worthiness through Christ even when times are tough. Humility makes you confident in the One who is in you. Humility is a super-power in the Kingdom.

Humility and timidness are not the same thing. Being truly humble means being powerful.

Only by going through God's threshing floor will you become the woman He has created you to be, sanctified to the Lord. Exodus 29:1 says, "This is the ceremony you must follow when you consecrate Aaron and his sons to serve me as priests: Take a young bull and two rams with no defects" (NLT). Consecration leads to sanctification. Sanctification means being set apart for the exclusive use of God.

As you look back on the time of tribulation, you will see how the process of threshing turned grain into flour for bread, for nutrition. Your sanctification process will make you usable to God. You will develop a holy fear of Him and love Him deeply. You will see His mighty hand in the trials, and you will magnify Him for His goodness in the midst of them.

The fear of the Lord does not mean you're scared of Him. As you acknowledge His goodness and His protection, you are in awe of who He is and what He can do.

Bring Forth the Treasure Within

When you undergo the pressure of the threshing floor, what is in you will come out. The stripping process gives you deeper insight. You understand that you did not bring about the harvest. The field doesn't thresh itself.

A pearl is a grain of sand that causes irritation inside a mollusk. To bring the gem out of you, some irritation will be required.

But you do not have to go through it alone. God will see you through it.

No grain was ever threshed while it was lying on the ground undisturbed. If you want to be set apart for the Greatest Craftsman, you must be ready to be tossed, stripped, and crushed. You will not be destroyed, but you will be purified. God will make great bread from your life that others will eat and be filled with.

You are also the yeast that God will use. On its own, yeast is worthless. But when it's placed into dough, it makes the dough rise. A small amount of yeast affects the entire loaf. You are meant to spread the Kingdom of God and His word of grace.

The enemy wants you to render your purpose useless. But if you make the decision every day to continue to pursue your God-given destiny, the flesh will continue to die. So embrace the preparation season.

The Preparation of Esther

Esther spent a year being prepared for her marriage to the king. For the first six months she was covered with bitter oils, and for the remaining six months she was doused with sweet nard. During this time, God was also preparing her.

The bitter oils represent suffering, purification, and cleansing. The sweet nard represents reward and glory.

Esther came from a Jewish family and was an orphan raised by her cousin Mordecai. God placed this woman in the palace of Persia, where she found favor with the king, and she was used to save the Jewish people.

After her preparation season, Esther took her position. You must do the same.

God orchestrated circumstances that are unique in His blueprint for your life. Consider who you are and where you are, then take courage to do what you must to influence the powers around you.

The process Esther went through was not easy. It was probably painful. But it made her strong enough to say, "I will do this. And if I die, I die" (Esther 4:16.)

God put people around Esther to help her fulfill her purpose. He will do the same for you. You will partner with those who have already gone through the threshing floor. You will make daily decisions to build courage.

The testing will be different as you grow in Christ. The higher you go, the more endurance, steadfastness, and patience you need. God wants you to be strong for what He has in store for you. He needs you not to buckle under pressure. That's why He's building muscle in you.

This is how the body of Christ is built, when we all come together in one Spirit. When self dies, only Christ remains. In order for anything to be built, a team is required. That team must be able to operate under pressure. They cannot quit when things get complicated. They must come together as one force.

Declaration

Because I have sown in tears, I will reap in joy. I will rejoice in His Word as I see the new day dawning.

CHAPTER SEVEN

KINSHIP

Now therefore ye are no more strangers and foreigners, but fellow citizens with the saints, and of the household of God. (Ephesians 2:19)

*K*INSHIP REFERS TO a blood relative with whom you share certain characteristics. You have been crafted into a royal bloodline by the blood of Jesus. In the Kingdom of God, we are all kin. We are born-again brothers and sisters. We are family.

We are also His body. Each of us is a different part, yet we need one another to function. As we go through His threshing floor, we are brought closer to the Greatest Craftsman. As a result, we are also woven more closely to our kin.

The Currency of Heaven

Relationship is the currency of heaven, and it is a

fundamental human need. We can't exist without it. We were created for a relationship with God and with other humans.

God's deep desire is to have a relationship with each of us. He sent His Son so that we can come back into a relationship with Him.

In the Old Testament, the tabernacle was very important. It was where God came to dwell in the midst of His people. Now we are His temple, and He dwells in us. He redeems us, restores us, and washes us as we read His word and spend time with Him. He fortifies our identity in Him as we go deeper into Him and seek more of Him.

Love is key in any relationship. The more you know God, the more deeply and passionately you will love Him. This divine relationship will stretch you, and you will see more of Jesus in you as you grow in Him.

We all need each other too. We were not created to do life alone. As Scripture says, "Iron sharpens iron" (Proverbs 27:17). You need someone who will lift your arms in battle when you grow weary. They will need you to do the same for them when they feel like they can't go on any longer. But before we can carry another's burdens, we must first put ours down. That requires divine love.

Associations

You probably know hundreds of people, but only a few are your close friends, individuals you hang out with and bond with.

All of your friends, family members, and co-workers have a direct bearing on your self-esteem. If you are around highly influential people, you have a strong chance of success because you are learning their values and principles, which will help you grow as a person.

If your associates don't care about anything but living a carefree life, you will be influenced to adopt their beliefs. If you go out all the time and don't take care of yourself, you will end up sick. If you ignore the important things in life, that can lead to undesirable consequences.

Your associations have a direct bearing on your physical and emotional health. If you associate with positive people, you have a good chance of being happy. A true friend is someone you can reach out to when you're experiencing troubling times, not someone who makes things worse by making light of your problems.

The people you hang out with affect your mental well-being and self-esteem as well. So surround yourself with people who bring out the best in you. Don't let anyone or anything ruin those valuable relationships.

If you don't have any special friends right now, ask God to bring people to you who will genuinely care about you and will push you to raise the bar so that you can reach your potential.

Everyone you know has a role to play in your life. You can learn from them or they may learn from you. We all have something that another person needs.

At various times in your life, some relationships will be maintained while others end. Pay attention to the season you are in and the people who are walking with you in it.

Rahab

In the book of Joshua, we read about Rahab, a woman who left everything she ever knew and chose God.

Rahab was a harlot who lived in Jericho, and she knew that God was with the Israelites. She believed in the power of God, Creator of all things. She realized that if she wanted a brighter future, she would have to make some sacrifices.

When two Israelite spies came to scout out the

city prior to their attack, Rahab chose to protect the men, even though that meant cutting herself off from everything she knew.

No matter who you are, if you know those who follow God, live in their culture, and collaborate with them, God will operate on your behalf.

Rahab's connection with the two Israelite spies was a divine appointment for her and her family. Both parties benefitted. The Israelites received help from within the city to defeat their enemy, and Rahab's family was saved.

As a result of her decision that day, Rahab became the wife of Salmon. Salmon had a son named Boaz, who married a woman named Ruth, and their offspring became the bloodline of our Savior, Jesus. Wow!

In John 6:64–71, we see that not all who followed Jesus truly believed. He chose twelve men to be His personal friends, but He knew that one would betray Him. Many may follow you because of what you are doing in a season of life, believing they have the same assignment you do. But not all will believe in you, and some may not stay with you.

You may have a Judas among your close personal connections. But don't be discouraged. Even this relationship has a purpose in your life.

You may not be able to achieve your goal without this betrayal. It might be setting you up to complete your task so that you can advance to a higher level.

The good news is that God will prepare you for that moment. When it comes, you will hurt. But eventually you will realize this circumstance was necessary.

Lean on God and big things will happen in your life. Let Him use you in whatever way He chooses, and He will take you to places you never knew you could go and show you His glory in remarkable ways.

The Right Brethren for the Assignment

God has given you the right people to collaborate with you in order to perform your assignment and execute His plans. There may be many or only a few. Be careful who you take along on your journey.

The Lord told Gideon there were too many people with him, and He couldn't give him victory over the Midianites because he and his soldiers would end up boasting that they'd succeeded by their own strength. So He instructed Gideon to tell his men that anyone who feared must go home. Twenty-two thousand soldiers went back, leaving him with only ten thousand. Yet that was still too many. God told him to take the men to drink water from a brook, and the ones who cupped their hands to drink would be the ones he kept. Only three hundred men cupped their hands.

Only those who truly revere the presence of God should partner with you. Those who honor Him and know the seriousness of His Kingdom will move forward with you and defeat the foe of this season in your life.

Gideon went from thirty-two thousand men to three hundred. Yet he did not question how God was going to defeat the enemy with such a small number. I'm sure he must have had doubts, maybe a certain level of fear. But his trust in God was much greater than that fear.

Your closest friends are your holy knights, order keepers, and protectors. They are to keep a watchful eye over you, always vigilant to detect any evil act that might taint or darken your realm. They constantly seek more training and knowledge to make themselves stronger and more capable. You will not find success in your purpose until you surround yourself with such associates.

Joshua 1:14–15 says, "Your wives, your little

ones, and your cattle, shall remain in the land which Moses gave you on this side Jordan; but ye shall pass before your brethren armed, all the mighty men of valour, and help them; Until the Lord have given your brethren rest, as he hath given you, and they also have possessed the land which the Lord your God giveth them: then ye shall return unto the land of your possession, and enjoy it, which Moses the Lord's servant gave you on this side Jordan toward the sunrising."

God brought people together, and all were promised their own land, but they were to help one another. No one could take possession of his land until they all worked together to defeat the enemy.

A kinship war is an exciting time of fellowship among family members. Many relatives will gather together for battle and show their might to all. No one can escape it, not even the newbies. All kin must stick together and fight side by side.

God has brought many associates into my life who helped me achieve my divine purpose. He used several pastors by having them invite me to preach. He used my uncle to take me into other nations to share the gospel. He used a powerful prophetess to break negative things off my life and activate what was in me. Many other brothers and sisters have come into my life to help me and be part of my journey. I hold all of these people dear to my heart. I even love those who betrayed me and I thank God for them, for they too served a purpose. All brothers and sisters in the Kingdom of God must work together so that we can all reach our Promised Land.

Knitted in Kinship

Godly leaders will train, disciple, and teach you. This will benefit all of the people you come in contact with as you model Christ for them. Those relationships will build a healthy culture.

But you must take action, and do the work of the ministry. Don't wait. You can't afford to miss this, and you may not have tomorrow. Rise up now to equip the saints so that the world can see the ministry of Jesus Christ.

The foremost person you need to knit yourself with is the Greatest Craftsman. He brought you into His kinship bloodline. As you become better acquainted with Him and come into intimacy with Him, you will see yourself through His loving eyes. He will make your heart leap when you sense Christ within other people. The Holy Spirit will confirm that the dream you are envisioning is from the Lord.

Declaration: *I am an inheritor of the Kingdom of God; therefore, He will bring people to me who will work alongside me to fulfill His purpose in my life. Lord, open the way for them to find me.*

CHAPTER EIGHT

IMAGINATION MADE REALITY

No man can rise above self-image. (Joel Osteen)

GOD HAS CRAFTED creative potential in you. There is an ocean of possibilities He wants you to explore. He has more for you than you could ever imagine or think of. So don't be afraid to imagine the impossible.

Creative Potential

In the business world, success is achieved by people who have a good self-image. The same is true in the spiritual realm and everything else in life. If you believe yourself to be worthy and powerful because of God's Spirit in you, there will be no room for doubt.

Picture yourself walking into God's creation

room, where all of His instruments and equipment are kept. You watch Him create something you have never seen before. Then He hands it to you.

But in order to use that gift, you need to see yourself as God does. Your outward appearance is just a shell, but it holds great potential.

Who do you think you are? What do you imagine yourself to be? Now consider who you are in Christ. You are reborn into the incorruptible seed. You can bear tremendous fruit from that seed. You have all the power and authority of Christ when you become one with Him. There is nothing He cannot do.

Envision through the Seed of Your Kind

Genesis 1:11–12 (NIV) tells us:

God said, "Let the land produce vegetation: seed-bearing plants and trees on the land that bear fruit with seed in it, according to their various kinds." And it was so. The land produces vegetation: plants bearing seed according to their kinds and trees bearing fruit with seed in it according to their kinds. And God saw it was good.

Meditate on these verses and apply them to your life. Sow the seed of your own kind, which is Jesus Christ, and see what kind of fruit you bear. You are meant to produce. God wants you to produce, to expand the Kingdom of the seed of Christ. And the Greatest Craftsman has already given you everything you need.

If you aren't producing, you are like the man in the parable who was given a talent and buried it in the ground. Because he feared he would lose it, the talent was taken from him and given to the man who multiplied his talents the most. Don't bury your talent because you have doubts or a low self-image. Remember, you are the image of Christ. You are part of His seed.

God gives each of us talents according to our ability. They are His property, and He wants us to do something with them. And He will bless it.

Dream Wrapped in a Seed

Every dream God has placed within you begins with a seed and has the potential to produce something. God gave you that dream so that you can make it a reality. He has already given you everything you need to cultivate the seed. Like an acorn contains the blueprint for a mighty oak, your dream seed has the potential to be something amazing.

What kind of harvest are you going to reap? Have you dropped your seed or forgotten about it, causing you to forfeit your harvest? Pick it back up and plant it.

As you pursue the dreams God gives you, don't expect everything to go smoothly and nothing bad to happen. Some of your dreams might seem impossible right now. But that doesn't mean they aren't part of God's plan. Don't give up if things aren't working out the way you expected. Keep that dream planted in the soft ground of your heart, and water it every day with the Word of God.

Water Your Seed

A planted seed needs a lot of water. The water of expectation will make your dream grow strong and beautiful. Expect God to do His part, for He always will.

In order to see fruit from your seed, you must water with patience and perseverance. Every seed produces differently. Some take a few months to grow. Others may not break through the ground for years, but when they do, they spring up quickly and grow at an astonishing rate.

What you think about your dream affects how

your seed will grow. If you believe in your dream, you will reap what you sow.

Keep a Record of Your Seed

Visualize your goal in your mind until you see it physically come to pass. Write down the details of your dream, and put it somewhere that you will see every day.

The Bible tells us that without a vision, people perish (Proverbs 29:18). If you see the details of your dream regularly, you will feel optimistic about it. It will be your ambition and motivation for life—what gets you up in the morning and motivates you to do more than just survive another day.

Writing it down will also help keep you accountable. You will ask yourself, *What am I watering the seed with? Am I watering it enough?* As you keep a record of the progress of your seed, God will reveal to you other ways to water and nurture it.

War with Praise and Worship Over Your Seed

The dream seed will take root, even when you can't see it. It must go beyond the surface and deep within you in order to fertilize the ground on your journey. So praise the Lord God Almighty, dance before Him, and watch Him cause that seed to grow.

For your dream to become a reality, you need to hear from God. Each morning when you wake up, tell Him you need to hear from Him. Then rest assured that you are proceeding in the right direction, because God's path for you cannot be mistaken.

In times of confusion, worship and praise God with your life. Praise and worship are not for the eyes and ears of others, but for God. The Greatest Craftsman is worthy to be worshiped, praised, and glorified. For every moment we're alive on earth, God deserves all of our hearts and all of our praise.

When you praise the Lord, do not hold back. Surrender your all to Him. Move forward as though your dream has already happened. Believe that what you're saying is true.

Decree Over Your Seed

Decree the promise of God over your dream seed. Speak words of faith. Instead of looking at your problems, declare what God has given you as a promise. Take the authority given to you by your Creator. Rise as a warrior, but also as a king and a priest.

Open your mouth and release the Word of God into the atmosphere. Words have power. The Bible says the power of the tongue is life and death (Proverbs 18:21). Your declaration will determine the direction of your life.

There is a time to speak and a time to be silent (Ecclesiastes 3:7). This is the time to speak. Do not keep silent, for the enemy wants to steal that seed by keeping you quiet. Bring that dream to life by taking your seat next to Christ and declaring what He has said about your seed.

Speak to that mountain and declare victory over it. He is more powerful than whatever is holding back the manifestation of your dream.

Unwavering Faith Sustains the Seed

Faith is the bridge between what is possible to achieve and the realization of that dream. We all possess the power of faith, but for most people it's greatly underutilized. Faith can change the world. But not everyone has faith in God. Some put their faith in money, material things, or relationships. But I encourage you to put your faith in the Greatest Craftsman. After all, He is the composer of your life. He already knows everything you need and has already made it available to you. You just have to reach out and grab it, with faith.

Faith is important when you dream. It creates opportunities, and then you can take advantage of them.

What would happen if everyone in the world had faith in the Greatest Craftsman? Faith can even be used to get you to a place where God's presence, power, and blessing are increased in your life. Faith allows you to receive the impossible. If it aligns with God's plan for your life.

The book of Hebrews says that faith is the substance of things hoped for and the evidence of things not seen (11:1). People who are filled with God's presence believe in miracles. By faith, they have seen their God-given dreams come to reality. They walk into places that are bigger than themselves because of what Jesus has said to them.

You can't enter the faith realm with your natural mind. You have to stop thinking logically, as you do in the natural world. Entering this realm requires humility, action, and a realization of how much God loves you.

God has given you an amazing idea, dream, or vision. Plant the seed of it in your mind. Water it with thoughts about what it will be. Think about how big this thing has the potential to become. Dream big. Then dream even bigger. Walk it out to completion with faith.

Dreaming with Eyes Wide Open

Numbers 24:4 refers to "the prophecy of one who hears the words of God, who sees vision from the Almighty, who falls prostrate, and whose eyes are opened" (NIV). Picture your perfect dream reality in this imperfect world. Believe that it's possible for what God has put into your heart to come to fruition. Let faith be added to the soil. Then watch that seed of a dream grow into a great thing.

When imagination turns into reality, the potential becomes kinetic! God imagined you before He formed you in your mother's womb. Now imagine yourself as the person He created you to be.

Don't put limits on what God has given you. That seed is capable of growing into a great thing if you take the steps to make it happen and believe! Let yourself go into the unknown. Don't be afraid of the waves. Keep your eyes on Jesus, and step into the waters.

Ocean of Possibilities

The ocean is one of the most misunderstood aspects of nature. The depths of the sea hold great mysteries. The same is true of your spiritual womb and the potential that is open to you. Take the initiative to explore the possibilities. God has a lot in store for you. You have much to find and uncover.

Look deep. Do not let your dream be lost at sea Ask the Greatest Craftsman to enable you to see what He has crafted for you. Take a risk and dive in with the Holy Spirit, allowing Him to show you the secrets of your Creator. Let Him reveal to you the uniqueness of your life, and let Him endow you with the power to see it come true.

Pilot's wife had a dream that God gave her to warn them about crucifying Jesus. She paid attention to it and told her husband about it.

Samuel's mother dreamed of having a son. That dream, placed within her by the Creator, remained unfulfilled for many years. But she did not let go of that dream. She went to her Creator every day and cried out to Him. Finally her prayer was answered. She brought forth the prophet Samuel, who served the Lord all his life. Samuel's mother's story shows how God's purpose arises, even from a barren place.

God Fulfills in Barrenness

In Isaiah 41:18–20, God says, "I will open rivers in high places, and fountains in the midst of the valleys: I will make the wilderness a pool of water, and the dry land springs of water. I will plant in the wilderness the cedar, the shittah tree, and the myrtle, and the oil tree; I will set in the desert the fir tree, and the pine, and the box tree together. That they may see, and know, and consider, and understand together, that the hand of the Lord hath done this, and the Holy One of Israel hath created it."

God can make something out of nothing. His supernatural power can fill the most barren place in the natural world.

You may think you are barren, but God will bring your dream to life with vibrant colors, full of flowers that will produce beautiful seeds that will multiply. It's not too late for you to come out of your barren place.

God works in empty spaces. According to Genesis 1:1–2, "In the beginning God created the heaven and the earth. And the earth was without form, and void; and darkness was upon the face of the deep. And the Spirit of God moved upon the face of the waters."

If you don't give up on what God has placed in your heart, you will come into a deeper knowledge of your identity in Christ. God will awaken the womb where you will incubate your dream. You will be like Sarah and Elizabeth, who in old age bore the purposes and plans of the Great I AM.

The first step to achievement is an idea. The second step is a plan of action. The third step is physical activity on the plan. The mind never moves without first being stimulated. Work out the muscle of your imagination. The more you use it, the stronger it will become. Stimulate what God has given you as a dream, and then carry it out into action.

Declaration

I will keep my thoughts continually fixed on what is authentic and real, honorable and admirable, beautiful and respectful, pure and holy, merciful and kind. I will fasten my thoughts on every glorious work of God, praising Him always. (See Philippians 4:8 TPT.) I believe that my God-given dreams will manifest into reality.

CHAPTER NINE

CARRY INTO ACTION

Commit to the Lord whatever you do, and he will establish your plans. (Proverbs 16:3 NIV)

YOU HAVE BEEN placed into your family, your city, your nation, your business, your relationships, and your ministries to bring about the plans of the Greatest Craftsman. Act on what He is calling you into. Critical thinking will be required for you to carry it out.

Prolong No More

Time and life are short. If God has called you to do something, do it. He has given you the keys of authority.

In the book of Numbers, Zelophehad had five daughters but no son. In that time, a family's land could only be distributed to a male (27:1–4). When Zelophehad passed away, his land was to be distributed to other tribes.

His daughters knew that if they did not take action, their father's name would be forgotten among God's people. So they walked into the Jewish council of men to make their voices heard. They took action and brought about a change in this unjust law.

Zelophehad's daughters fought for the name of their father. We should also take action and fight for our Father's name.

Time to Leave the Wilderness

If you are in a wilderness, stop wandering around like the Israelites. If you don't, forty days of hesitation will turn into forty years of regret. Make the decision. Then take action.

Learn from the mistakes of the Israelites. God delivered them from Egypt, but then they had to shift their mindset. Even after they were delivered, they were still captive in their minds.

God performed miracles, signs, and wonders in their midst. He spoke to them and dwelled with them. Yet they complained, rebelled, and doubted due to their unbelief. One decision resulted in an action that caused them to miss their promised inheritance.

If they had thought about everything God had done for them, their minds would have been at rest, knowing that God had not abandoned them and that He would lead them to triumph. They would have taken appropriate action and would have possessed the Promised Land.

I Hope to or I Will

Hoping for something is a start, but it's not enough to achieve change or make dreams reality. To truly succeed, however, there should be calculated actions in order to materialize those lofty expectations.

In Judges 9, when Abimelech came to a city with the intent to destroy it, the people fled to a strong tower within the city. Abimelech tried to burn the tower, but one woman took action. She did not just sit in her home, hoping for someone to come rescue them or praying that no harm would come to her loved ones. She took matters into her own hands. She broke Abimelech's skull.

Has the spirit of Abimelech come into your city looking to destroy it, you and your family? Even if you are in the strong tower of the Lord, where

He protects you, you must take action. Break the skull of the enemy, Satan, so that God can bring freedom to you and all of your loved ones. Don't be afraid. You can do this. And with God, you will.

The Leap Is Worth the Risk

Make a bold and courageous move. Take your strong position. God has chosen to partner with you to bring His purpose on the earth. But you must be intentional.

You have been called to bring justice into the land. It is time to prepare for your defense.

You were born on a battlefield. So fight the war! The coming event will set the course of the future. At a unique moment in time, your choice will define your life. You must perceive that moment quickly. If you don't, your atmosphere will change, and you will become barren.

When Esther's time had come, she needed to move swiftly. Her decision would affect all of her people. The action she took would change the course of history.

Be bold and courageous like Esther. Take action. The future is in your hands. Bring to light what is hidden in secret. Take advantage of every day. Spend your life with purpose.

Rahab is another woman who took a bold and

courageous stand. In the book of Hebrews, we read the account of her faith in God, witnessed by her actions. In one moment, her decision changed the course of her destiny and purpose.

God used Rahab to bless the nation of Israel. He put her in that time and place to raise her up as a leader, someone who would take matters into her own hands for her family's sake.

Taking action like Rahab means you are exercising your faith.

Crafted as a Leader

God is crafting you to become a leader. You are an instrument in God's hand. You are not ordinary. God has prepared you. Like Esther's king, He has granted you the ability to come in contact with His scepter. He is waiting for you to draw closer. His ears are attentive to your petition. He will act on your behalf. He welcomes you at His table and listens to what you have to say. Take action by entering your prayer closet and spending time with Him. Approach His throne with your petition. He wants to work with you as a partner.

God will use you to bring justice into your situation as you take action to lead with the mind of Christ. He will use you to repair and rebuild, as He used the daughters of Shallum, who helped repair the wall of Jerusalem. Nehemiah 3:8 says they were like the men who drove cattle. They did whatever was necessary to help rebuild what had been broken down for so long. They thought like leaders, unlike all the other women of their day.

You are the repairer of the breach. Everything that has kept you from entering into the presence of God will be removed. You will be reunited with the Greatest Craftsman in this season. You have come to rebuild the house of the Lord, which has been sitting in desolation for too long.

God is listening for your *yes*. He is waiting for you to take action. Nothing will happen if you don't work at it. Be like the ant, which is always working and preparing. Dreaming without a strategy is just wishful thinking. If you want to make a lasting impact on the lives of others, think about what it will take to get there. Then put your plan into action. Become the leader God has called you to be.

Declaration

I will go from stagnant living to thriving. I am preparing my mind for action, and being sober-minded, I set my hope fully on the grace that will be brought to me at the revelation of Jesus Christ according to 1 Peter 1:13.

CHAPTER TEN

RISE, MUSING WOMAN LEADER

Strength and honour are her clothing; and she shall rejoice in time to come. (Proverbs 31:25)

MUSING MEANS "MEDITATION." A musing woman leader meditates on the Kingdom of God. Whether you're a stay-at-home mom, an author, a waitress, a musician, or an artist, God has placed you where you are to influence those around you and reshape the way they think.

You won't be able to do that if you are led strictly by your emotions and your earthy intellect. Do not rely on your own understanding. Ask the Greatest Craftsman to show you His thoughts. As He drops revelations into your soul, your eyes will be opened. Barriers will come down, scales will fall off your eyes, and prison doors will be unlocked. Even if you don't feel it, if you continue to trust, He will work in your life.

God doesn't want us to be passive, but to act. Don't sit around thinking, *If it is God's will, it'll happen.* You have a part to play. Go for it, in Jesus's name. Get yourself into a proactive mentality.

In Judges 4:9, God gave Sisera into the hands of Jael, the wife of Heber, who was not an Israelite. She used her quick thinking and took a fearless stand, without hesitation or doubt. Perhaps Jael had habitually practiced this type of thinking and that's why the Lord used her for this triumph.

As you move in this mentality for God's Kingdom, He will use you to bring about victory.

The Greatest Craftsman is preparing you for the moment when He will hand over the enemy into your presence. You will triumph over him if you answer that call. You are going to be a conqueror in the combat ahead. Do not let fear or doubt stop you from doing great things for the Lord.

We are living in critical times, so we need critical strategies. Become like a child and observe everything around you. Seek the wisdom of God so that you can be the gateway to the house of the Lord.

God's favor has come upon women for the

end of days. He is extending His grace to you right now. He will give you lofty ideas and problem-solving skills. Wealth will be your portion, and you will use this currency to extend the Kingdom of the Greatest Craftsman.

You will become the musing leader who will shift the thoughts of those who have been deceived by lies. You will break the strongholds of minds that are being oppressed by the enemy. Many are trapped right now, but you will arise to bring breakthroughs. You have been placed in your spheres of influence to draw people into the truth and turn their worlds upside down.

Without Christ, you are nothing, but you have the Great I AM within you. He is greater than any human, and He can do mighty things. Nothing is impossible for Him. You are empowered by the Holy Spirit. You will succeed, not by your strength, but by the Spirit of God.

Partner with Wisdom

Proverbs 9:6 tells us to lay aside simple thoughts. We must listen to wisdom, especially for the times we are living in and the times that are coming. Guard your life with the revelation of the Creator.

God is blessing you with the anointing of Daniel. Daniel was considered wiser than all the magicians of Babylon because God revealed to him hidden secrets. Daniel 2:22 says, "He revealeth the deep and secret things: he knoweth what is in the darkness, and the light dwelleth with him." God will give you wisdom by revealing hidden things, too, and by that the world will know He is God and you are His.

The world is falling deeper into darkness, losing their sight and the ability to know what direction they are walking in. However, you will bring the light that will show them the way out of darkness like God did for Daniel. Daniel 2:48 says, "The king made Daniel a great man, gave him many great gifts, and made him ruler over the whole province of Babylon, and chief of the governors over all the wise men of Babylon." Verse 49 says he sat at the gate of the king. That is where God wants to put you as well.

Want to know how to receive divine wisdom? Proverbs 8:1–3 says:

> *Doth not wisdom cry? and understanding put forth her voice?*
>
> *She standeth in the top of high places, by the way in the places of the paths.*
>
> *She crieth at the gates, at the entry of the city, at the coming in at the doors.*

Wisdom is looking for someone who is ready to listen to her and learn from her. She is always speaking and calling.

Go up to Mount Zion, the house of God. Leave that mountain you've been dwelling in before it's too late (Deuteronomy 2:3). Follow Jesus, the Bright Morning Star. Keep yourself in the mountain where wisdom lives. Dwell with her as she empowers you to have an open mind. Receive the revelation of knowledge that will help you reign in your life.

The Greatest Craftsman promises you, according to Proverbs 8:6–7, that you will come out of wisdom's house with the gleam of the Lord shining on your face, and people will know that you have been in the Father's house. Be like Queen of Sheba, who left all she knew to seek the wisdom of King Solomon.

Many Kingdom entrepreneurs have been equipped to teach you, not only spiritually but also in the natural. Invest in yourself. You are more valuable than you realize.

Don't wait for the perfect timing. It may never come. The greatest opportunities arise from the hardships you find yourself in. Be like the widow who went to the prophet of God for help after her husband died (2 King 4:1). Her son was about to be taken from her to pay for his father's debt. The prophet asked her what she had, and she replied, "I have nothing but a jar of oil in my house." Yet she listened to the wisdom and instructions of the prophet and borrowed empty jars from her neighbors. She poured her small amount of oil into them, and the jars were supernaturally filled. She looked for more jars, but no more were available. Her obedience to the prophet was wise, for it gave her a breakthrough. She paid off her debt and became an entrepreneur, living off the remainder of the abundant oil she had.

If you do not seek the word of the Creator, the fountain of wisdom will not flow. We may go to church and ask the Lord to drench us in His river, but we must take action when we read His Word. Scripture is the water that can become rivers of life within you.

The enemy wants to shut your mouth by screaming fear and confusion into your mind. He wants to intimidate you, Christ's bride. However, a remnant is fighting for you, just as Samson did in the hillside of Lehi (meaning "jawbone") against the uncircumcised Philistines in Judges 15:18–19. Perhaps you have been declaring the Word of God but, like Samson, you have fought with all you have, and now you feel like you are close to dying. You are weary of all the enemies that have come against you. You feel dry and thirsty.

Cry out to God, for He will cause water to come out from the ground to revive your spirit. This water is hidden now, but God will break open the fountains to revive you.

At the cross, Jesus said He was thirsty. Soon after, He gave up His spirit. Then the curtain of the Holy of Holies was torn from top to bottom, and the foundations of God's living water burst out, making it available for all to drink from.

"By his divine revelation he broke open the hidden fountains of the deep, bringing secret springs to the surface as the mist of the night dripped down from heaven" (Proverbs 3:20 TPT). The Spirit of the Lord will come upon you like the dew on Mount Hermon. He will come from heaven to drench you with His refreshing presence.

Come into harmony with the Spirit of the Greatest Craftsman. "Harmony is as refreshing as the dew from Mount Hermon that falls on the mountain of Zion. And there the Lord has pronounced his blessings, even life everlasting" (Psalm 133:3 NLT).

"My doctrine shall drop as the rain, my speech shall distil as the dew, as the small rain upon the tender herb, and as the showers upon the grass..." (Deuteronomy 32:2).

Wait patiently. We all struggle with patience, but it is a fruit of the Spirit.

Ruth lay at the feet of Boaz all night waiting for his instruction. So shall it be with you. As the world gets darker, continue to lie at the feet of Jesus, waiting for Him to give you instructions for what to do. Be at peace and rely on Him. He will arise at the break of dawn and send you on your way with an abundant harvest.

Do not rush when you are with Jesus. Delight in His presence. Take time to get to know Him and His heart. For this is where you will hear His voice and His instruction clearly.

If you don't wait patiently on Him, you will rise up in your own wisdom, thinking you know what's best. You will do your own work and not what the Greatest Craftsman is calling you to do.

When you have heard Him, then come out of His chamber and move quickly. Do the best you can for Him. Then He will give you rest.

Do not be anxious about anything, but in everything give thanks (Philippians 4:6). The answer is coming.

In these last days, we need the manifold wisdom of the Lord. It will be even more necessary as the darkness grows. You can uphold His wisdom as you meditate on His Word. "Therefore whosoever heareth these sayings of mine, and doeth them, I will liken him unto a wise man, which built his house upon a rock..." (Matthew 7:24).

Do not be a foolish woman. "Fools find no pleasure in understanding but delight in airing their own opinions" (Proverbs 18:2). Instead be a woman full of wisdom. "Wisdom's instruction is to fear the Lord, and humility comes before honor" (Proverbs 15:33).

As the Greatest Craftsman takes you into your eternal purpose and identity, you will be filled with the rivers of His Word. They will overflow with life. This is necessary for taking possession of the land He wants to give you. To possess it, you must listen to His teachings.

The New Forerunner

Many women today have been influenced by culture, education, politics, and even religion. But God wants us to change the way we think. We must be intentional about it. If we sit with the Holy Spirit daily and meditate on Scripture, we will think deeper than the surface.

Changing from the inside out takes time, but it will happen if you persevere. People will notice a difference in you. And in your breakthrough,

God's power will be revealed. People's lives will be transformed as a result of your change. You will become the forerunner who leads people into shifting the way they think.

Because your way of thinking comes from heaven, the ways of man will not shake you. You will deliver people from their mental bondage that is keeping them from living freely in their God-given purpose.

Many have allowed the world's thinking to penetrate their minds. They have listened to the news, teachers, or loved ones who are not aligned with the thoughts of God. But you can take a stand and make way for a different way of thinking, one that surpasses all human understanding, for it will be the very thoughts of God.

Travail

When God creates something, it emerges from a state of emptiness. Sarah, Hannah, and Elizabeth were all barren women whom God utilized to bring forth something new on the earth. The one who was barren will give birth to a new move of the Greatest Craftsman.

So travail in intercession. Go after Jesus like the Canaanite woman who urged Him to heal her daughter who was possessed by demons. She did not leave Him alone even when others perceived her as being an annoying woman. She cried out for Him. Finally Jesus said, "Your faith is great," and He healed her daughter (Matthew 15:21–28).

Travail in worship and praise. Miriam praised God as she and the Israelites crossed the river. David danced in the open after God gave him victory. Anna the prophetess worshiped in the temple day and night with fasting and prayer. She prayed for many years, and due to her faithfulness, she saw Jesus the Messiah when He was eight days old. She was one of only two people who recognized Jesus in the temple at that time.

Keep travailing. The birth pains will only last a little while longer.

God has given women supernatural strength. The travail of childbirth is incomparable to any other pain. The only way women can endure such pain is by the grace of God given to them.

Suffering in childbirth is the curse that came upon us due to the sin that Eve brought into the world. But thanks to God's mercy, He gives us the ability to endure the pain.

I believe God has endowed women with grace to endure in the Spirit as well. The pain of travailing in the Spirit is severe as we fight off the principalities of this world. But God has given women the ability to endure in interceding.

Keep pushing in prayer with a contrite spirit. Remember, God's ways are not our own. They are much higher than ours. You may not know why some breakthroughs take a few days while others linger for years or even decades. But don't give up hope. If God said it, it will be completed. He is the same now as He was yesterday and will be forevermore (Hebrews 13:8).

Empty yourself so that He can fill you with His glory and power. Don't get stuck in your old thoughts. Let go of everything you know, and ask the Holy Spirit to show you new things He wants to bring forth upon the earth. What He did for all the barren women in His lineage He will do in your life. Everything can be utilized for His glory. And everything can contribute toward your good in some manner or another.

You are the waters, and the Holy Spirit is hovering over you. It may seem dark right now, but the light of Christ will shine to the depth of the darkness. The Holy Spirit is within you, and He is waiting for the appropriate moment to emerge upon you.

Your Current Location Is Not Permanent

You may have been in the driest desert or the darkest night. But you are not lost. God has a plan for you.

We are living in the end of days, where people call evil good and good evil (Romans 1:18-32). The body of Christ is being challenged and tested. People are full of themselves, chasing after their own desires with carnal minds. But it is not so with you, for you know there is more than the eye can see.

You are in the world but not of it (John 17:15-21). You are the perfect person for God's plan. You will come out of the valley, and He will fill you with His glory. The place you've been in has positioned you for the favor of God. For you are learning to depend fully on Him and to not be self-dependent.

Jesus was led into the wilderness by the Holy Spirit for forty days. He was tested and tried there. But when He came out, He emerged with power from heaven.

You may wonder why God has allowed you to be in the wilderness for so long. But you are learning to understand His greatness so that you can display His power to those around you.

Our confidence needs to be in Him, not in flesh or works. God does everything, and we just partner with Him.

The woman He is rising up for such a time as this is you. The Holy Spirit is incubating greatness within you. He is showing you your purpose, your call, your assignment. He is giving you hope and strength.

You are about to come out of that place where everything in you has been diluted. Like a butterfly, you will break out of that shell and spread your wings.

You are in the incubation stage now, but get ready! The Greatest Craftsman is about to bring you forth for the greatest move He has ever made.

Atmosphere Shifter

The company of women that God is establishing will emerge from the swamps to shift the atmosphere. God will bring forth a new thing.

Women in the Bible had a lot against them, but they stepped out boldly in faith.

The atmosphere you walk into may be full of oppression and depression, but you will carry peace and freedom with you. You will shift an atmosphere full of hopelessness and bitterness by bringing hope and joy. From longing to fulfillment, from darkness to light. From fear to courage, from shaking to stability, from lowliness to victory.

In the middle of a storm, Jesus commanded peace over the waters. So shall it be with you. The power to shift atmospheres is within you. Overcome the fear or resistance you feel.

Some won't like you if you are honest. You may be a threat to their ego or the status quo. But authenticity is the most important thing about you.

Fight to shape the world you live in by being true to your core nature. Speak out and declare what the Lord is saying. In the midst of pain and obstacles, be determined not to complain but to rise up. Do not panic, but face your enemy. Your life is covered with the glory of God. You won't just survive, but you will flourish as you stand on the promises of God.

Come to the well. He is waiting there for you. He will give you His water. You will trust Him more because of the encounter you will have with Him. Then tell others everything He has said to you. Tell it with joy, for He will set you free from every lie of the enemy. He will enthrone Himself in your mind. All who believe will shift because of the power of God that accompanies you wherever you go.

The barriers will come down as He rises up in you. Everything that has separated you from Him will be demolished. Everything that has kept you from entering into His fullness will disappear. Your identity will be fortified as you come to the knowledge of God, who is all knowing.

He is not done with you; He is only getting started. In all the tough times that may come, you will have victory in Him. You are a precious possession of the Greatest Craftsman. You can break through the limitations of this world. Don't confine yourself to what you see. Arise, for your light has come.

He who is the Bright Morning Star will arise within you as you yield to Him. He is the hope of your salvation, so you can take hope and strength to others. They will come to Him and you will be the door He uses. You will be the shining star He brings into someone's darkest night.

"The people who walk in darkness have seen a great light; on those who live in a land of deep darkness a light has dawned" (Isaiah 9:2).

You have a light within you that glorifies your Creator. Your light will lead many into righteousness. "Those who are wise will shine like the brightness of the heavens, and those who lead many to righteousness, like the stars for ever and ever" (Daniel 12:3). You will govern over the dark, for the moon that represents the bride and the stars that represent individuals in Christ govern over the kingdom of darkness. "The moon and stars govern the night; His love endures forever" (Psalm 136:9).

Godly women will move like pioneers to make changes in their homes, cities, government, education, and relationships as they transition into their rightful positions.

Women have sometimes been looked upon as the weaker sex. But God's eyes and heart have been upon women, and He works in their hearts and minds as He is raising them up to be the musing leaders of this age.

Proverbs 31 women are being prepared in the body of Christ to bring forth a new thing upon the earth. The men will join them and they will move hand in hand, for they will recognize that God is doing these things.

Crafted for Change

The Greatest Craftsman has gifted you with certain capabilities, characteristics, and abilities. You are not hasty or light-minded in judgment (Proverbs 14:5). You are capable of showing mercy, ruling a household, managing life's affairs, and lying on God's altar as an offering for service (1 Timothy 5:14). You are worthy to be called a woman of God. You are capable of ruling and reigning. You hold a place of honor and esteem in the Kingdom of God.

You were not created to be misused or abused. You were made by the Greatest Craftsman with purpose. The devil will attempt to devalue your identity, but don't let him convince you (2 Timothy 1:7). Believe what God says about you.

You are purposed by God just like Christ was (Romans 8:29). You were created for good works, so walk in them. You were made by God to be lavishly loved and used for good works (Ephesians 2:10). Jesus said you shall do greater things than He did (John 14:12). That is what He has purposed you for.

God will open up the waters in your desert place. "He turns a wilderness into a pool of water and dry ground into water springs" (Psalm 107:35). You may have been fighting the Philistines, and now you feel weary. You may have found deliverance from your enemies, but now you are thirsty and feel like you are losing your life. Cry out, and watch God bring water from the deep hollow to refresh and revive you. Feel the mist of the Spirit of God covering you.

God will turn your life around so that people will know that He has done it all for you.

Set the Stage for the Greatest Craftsman

Make the way clear for the King of Kings and His

glory will come. Every eye will see that He is the one true God. He will make every mountain low and every crooked place straight (Isaiah 40:4). You will proclaim the word of the Lord as His Spirit comes upon you. You will prepare the stage of the world, and every knee will bow to Him (Philippians 2:10).

Set the stage with the Good News, and the Spirit of God will call forth every son and daughter who belong to Him. They will see the Greatest Craftsman arise and stretch forth His mighty hand. He has chosen you to partner with Him to display His glory and majesty.

As the women prepared Jesus for His burial, He will use you to prepare for His coming. He will pour out His Spirit like never before.

Jesus came to shatter the power structure that had ruled in Jerusalem for so long. He taught with authority, knowing His words would spread across the world. He presented new ideas that were difficult for people to understand.

Jesus came to lead people out of their ignorance and into God's way of life (John 7:19). He was a liberator who came to free people from wrong beliefs, oppressive social structures, and spiritual blindness. And we have the same issues in our world.

Jesus said in Matthew 10:34, "I am not here to bring peace, but a sword." He has given this sword to you. Pick it up and go into the world. In Jesus's name, that sword will divide the darkness from light, the truth from the lie.

The Church today has become like the Pharisees. We have a perception of who God is, but we don't truly know Him. We have created a picture of Him in our minds that looks just like us. But Jesus said in John 8:23, "You are from below; I am from above. You are of this world; I am not of this world."

People are going along with the status quo and living in darkness. They see Jesus as a good person who tried to make a difference during His time on earth. But they're not interested in what He said. They care about their own righteousness, and Jesus came to change that.

You will share what God has revealed to you as you draw attention to the source of your learning: the Word of God. Search the Scriptures with passion. Do not be like the Pharisees, Sadducees, and other religious leaders of Jesus's time who thought they knew everything about the Scriptures. They were blinded by their religious traditions.

"You search the scriptures because you think they give you eternal life. But the scripture points to me" (John 5:39). Studying the Scriptures will ultimately reveal Jesus, the true Teacher.

Jesus debated with the Pharisees, Sadducees, and religious leaders, trying to get them to understand what God was doing in the world. You will do the same as you go about the Father's business.

As the Greatest Craftsman sets you into your eternal purpose and identity, you will be filled with the rivers of His Word and they will overflow with life. This life is necessary for possession of the land He promised. He gives us the land, but we must listen to His teachings before we can enter it.

The Lord says to you today what He told the Israelites in Deuteronomy 4:1: "Now therefore hearken, O Israel, unto the statutes and unto the judgments, which I teach you, for to do them, that ye may live, and go in and possess the land which the Lord God of your fathers giveth you." Reread this verse, putting your name in the places where it says "Israel." This is the word of the Lord that will change everything.

Don't wait any longer. Go in and take the land God has given you. Fight for it, removing all the enemies. Exercise the ability He has given you to be a musing leader.

Some giants have risen to try to keep you from your inheritance. Take that territory back, then expand it as far as you can. Do not fear persecution. When others come against you, you may feel the pain in your bosom like His mother, Mary, did. But keep pushing, for that will only last a moment before He arises and proves Himself mighty.

When Jesus rose in the resurrection, He told the women to go and tell others that He was alive. Today He will appear to any woman who comes looking for Him. And He will say, "Go tell them I am alive." The glory of God will cover the earth. So prepare the red carpet to welcome Him.

Declaration

Teach me to number my days, Lord, that I may gain a heart of wisdom (Psalm 90:12).

CONCLUSION

EPHESIANS 2:10 (TPT) SAYS, "We have become his poetry, a re-created people that will fulfill the destiny he has given each of us, for we are joined to Jesus, the Anointed One. Even before we were born, God planned in advance our destiny and the good works we would do to fulfill it!"

In God's divine poem for your life, He has crafted into you dreams and abilities that He will use for your purpose, which was prepared for you before you were even a thought in your parents' minds. As you grow in relationship with the Greatest Craftsman, you will become tightly knitted into your true identity. Your thoughts will be governed by Him and His creativity will flow through you. You will walk in your kinship rights with all of heaven. You will operate in your calling with confidence, knowing you are a new creation, reborn of the incorruptible seed, of a bloodline that is not of this world. You will be made whole as your genetic code is restored through Him.

Come to the threshing floor, knowing it will take you from glory to glory. You are going to mature to a level that will make you unshakable. You will stand firm no matter what. You will rise up, knowing the victory is already yours. You will inherit the land He has given you. As you come into your territory, you will take your rightful seat as a musing woman leader, and let the Greatest Craftsman come forth from within you.

ABOUT THE AUTHOR

JACQUIE R. MALDONADO is a wife and mother of three wonderful children. She has been commissioned by God to equip the Body of Christ with the tools they need to fulfill their destiny. Jacquie loves nothing more than seeing people come into their own power and knowing their identity in Christ. She is an encourager and a truth-teller, always looking to help others grow in their faith.

ENDNOTES

1. T. D. Jakes, *Woman, Thou Art Loosed* (Shippensburg, PA: Treasure House and Imprint of Destiny Image Publisher, 1994), 12–13.
2. James Strong, *The New Strong's Expanded Exhaustive Concordance of the Bible* (Nashville, TN: Thomas Nelson Publishers, 2010), 208.
3. Strong, 208.
4. Robert Proulx Heaney, https://www.britannica.com/science/bone-anatomy.
5. Strong, page 218.
6. Strong, page 218.
7. Strong, page 218.
8. Mark Barna, "New Analysis of Bone Helps Explain Why It's So Strong," *Discover* magazine, May 3, 2018, https://www.discovermagazine.com/health/new-analysis-of-bone-helps-explain-why-its-so-strong.
9. Winston Medical Center, https://www.winstonmedical.org/human-bones-joints-and-

muscles-facts/.

10. Charles Q. Choi, "Brute Force: Humans Can Sure Take a Punch," *LiveScience*, February 3, 2010, https://www.livescience.com/6040-brute-force-humans-punch.html.

11. Newton Desk, Why Human Bone (Femur) Is 4 Times Stronger Than Concrete - Health (newtondesk.com).

12. Cognifit, "Mirror neurons: The most powerful learning tool", https://blog.cognifit.com/mirror-neurons

13. W. E. Vine, *Vine's Complete Expository Dictionary of Old and New Testament Words* (Nashville, TN: Thomas Nelson, 1996), page122.

14. NEURONATION \ INTELLIGENCE AND IQ, MIND AND BRAIN, "Male vs. female brains – is there scientific evidence for our differences?", https://blog.neuronation.com/

15. Mark Wolum, It Didn't Start With You(New York, NY: Penguin Books,2017), page29

16. Need to cite the publication details for the source of this definition.

For infromation on bulk ordering this title, visit :

TALLPINEBOOKS.COM